The Sock Coloring Book

A Coloring Book for Adults

Amity Little

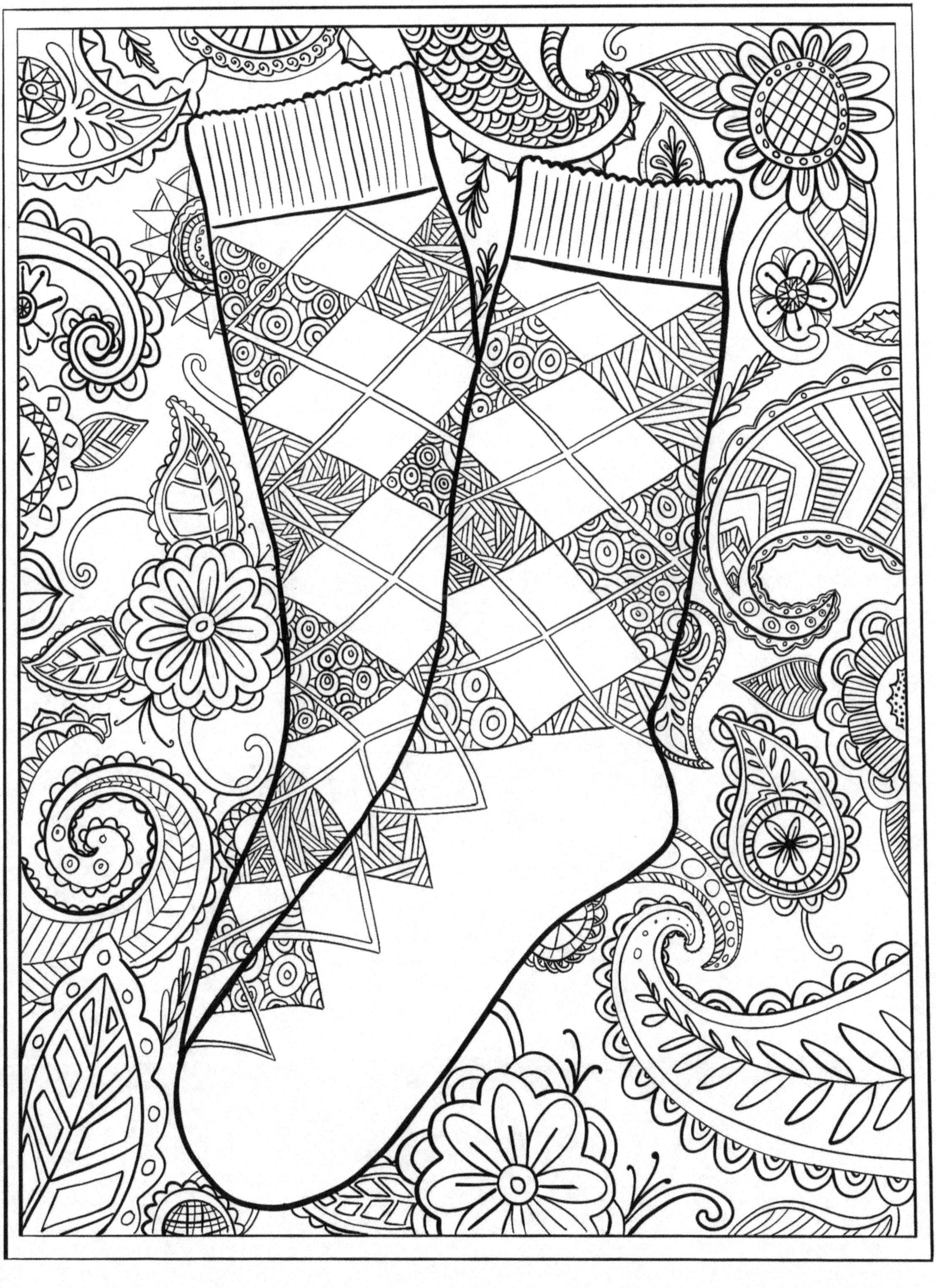

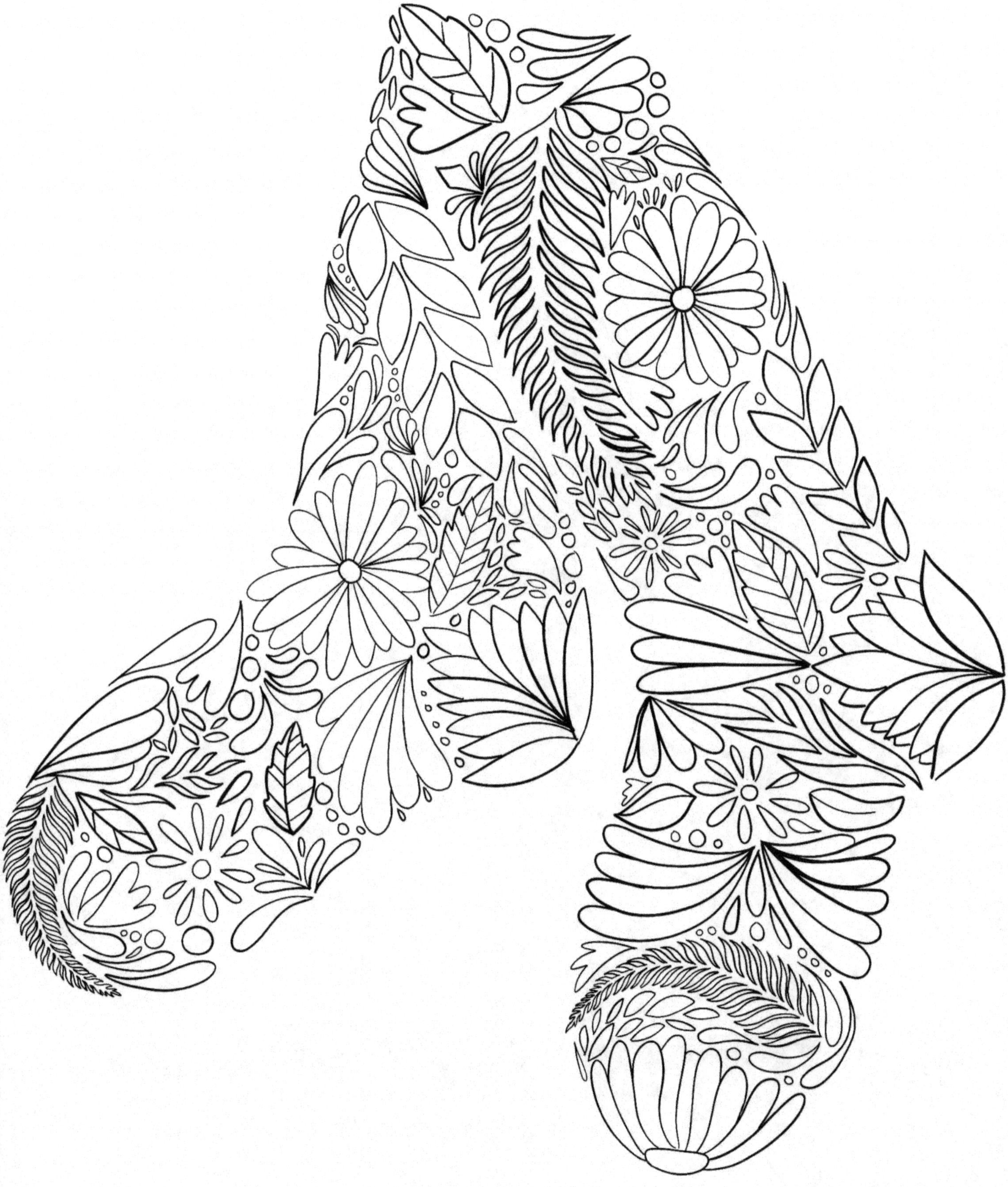

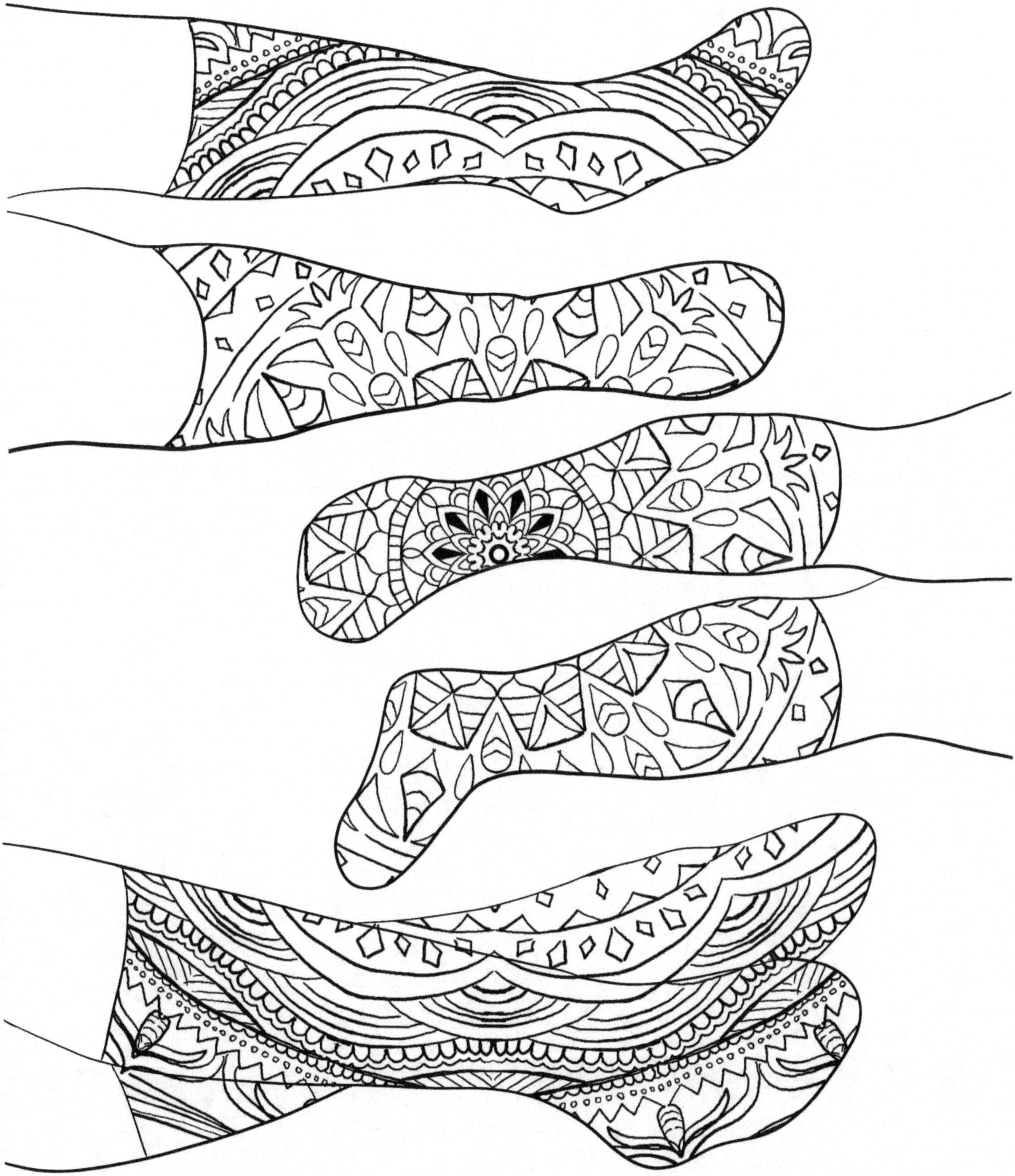

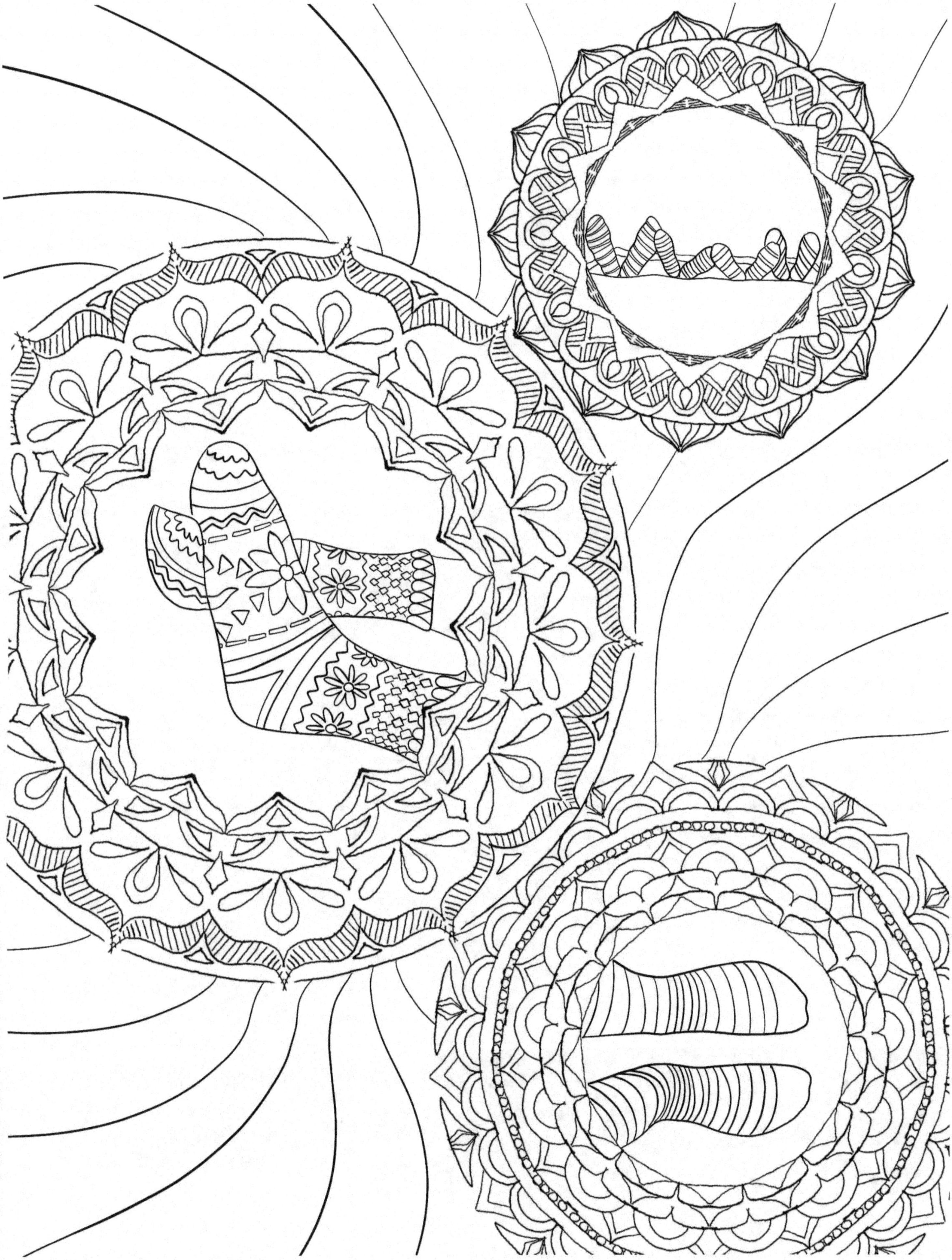

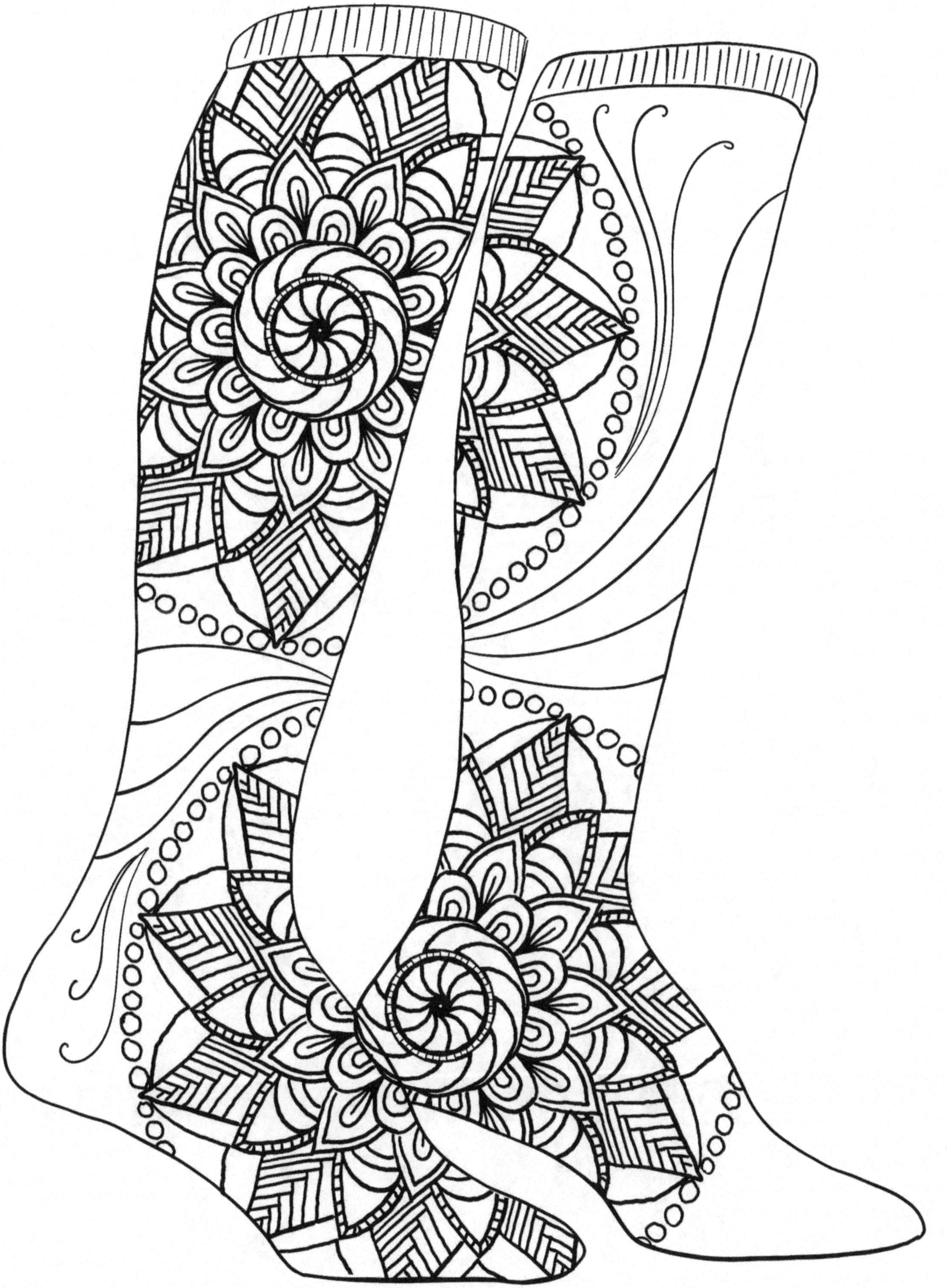

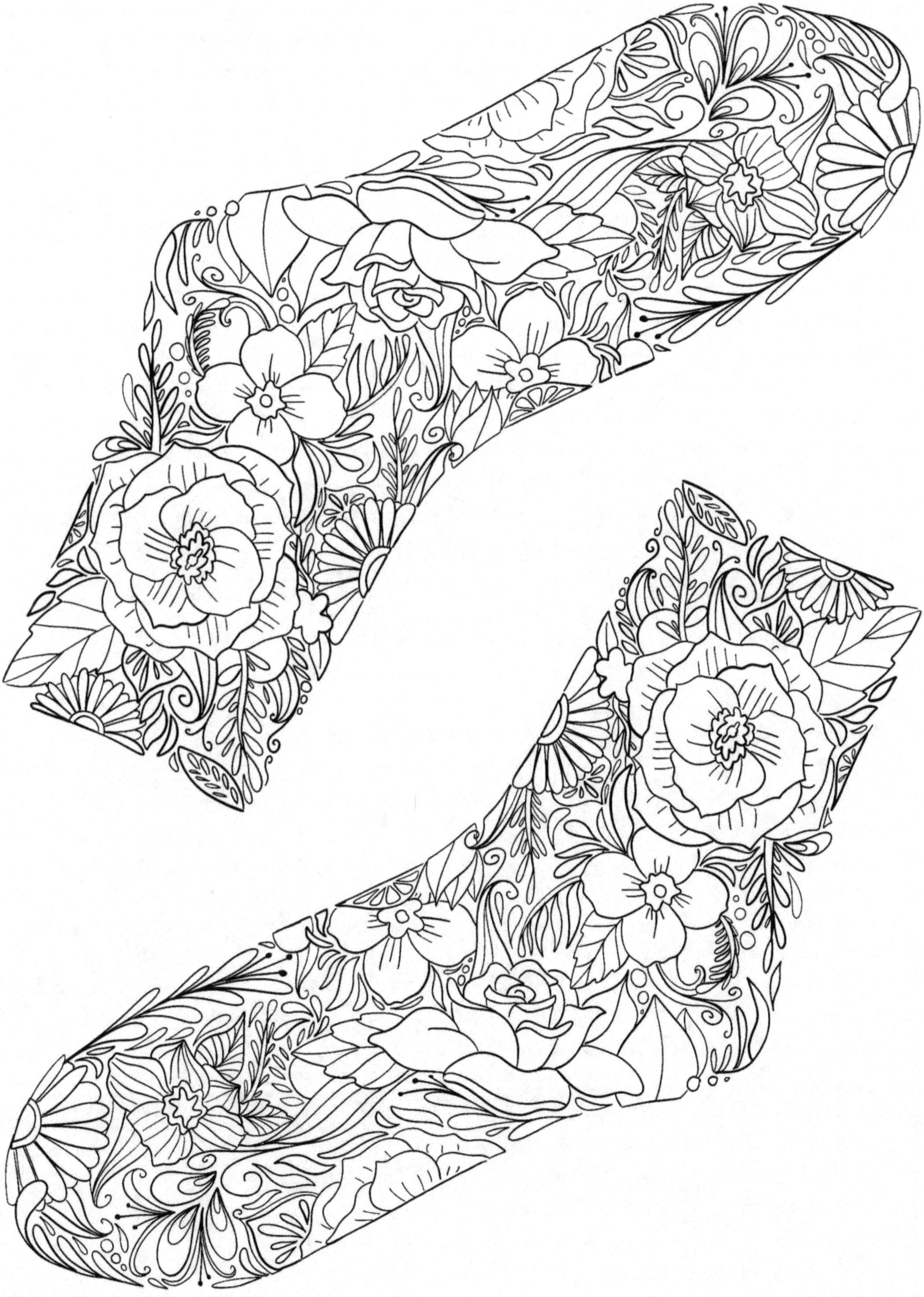

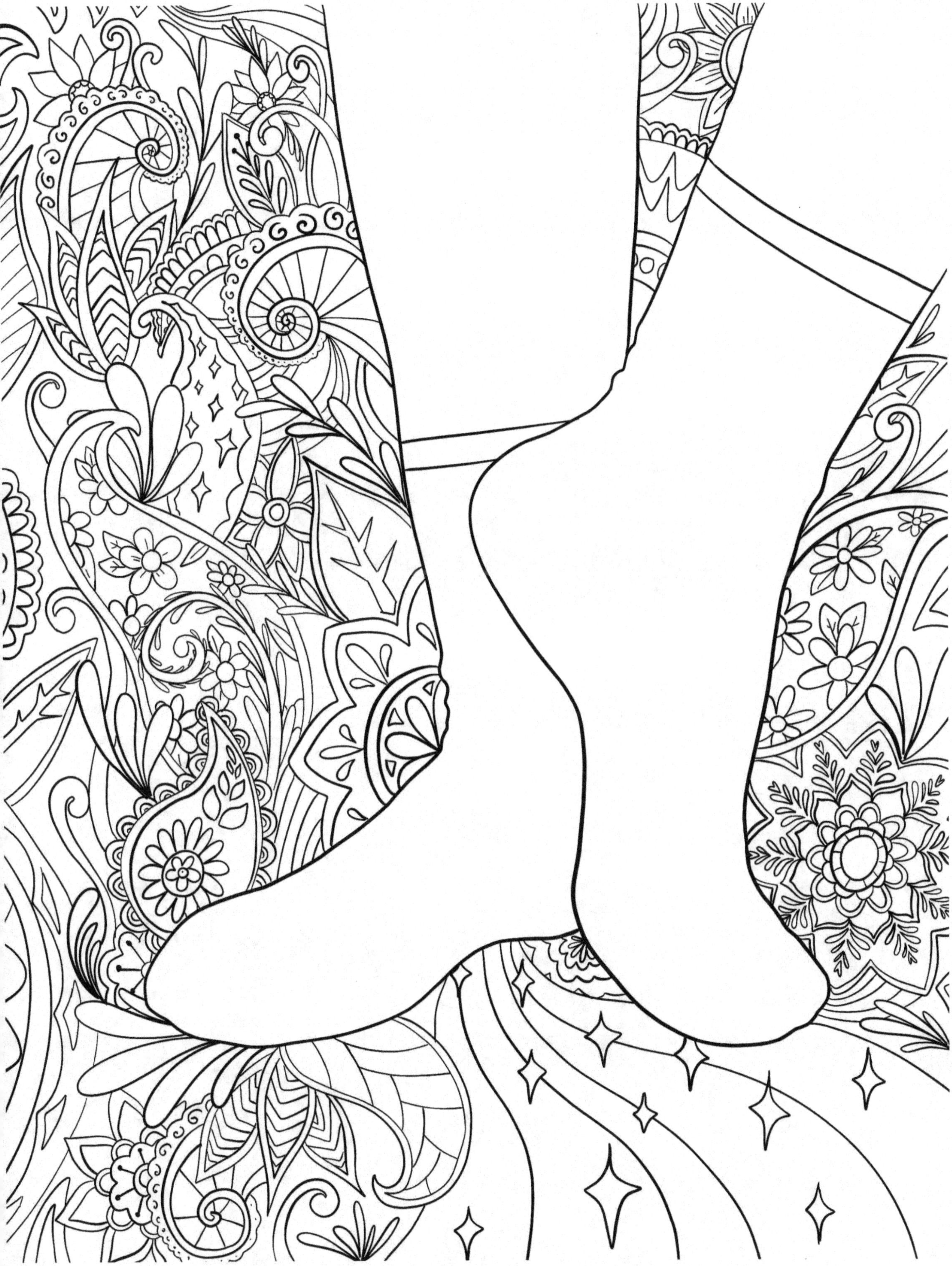

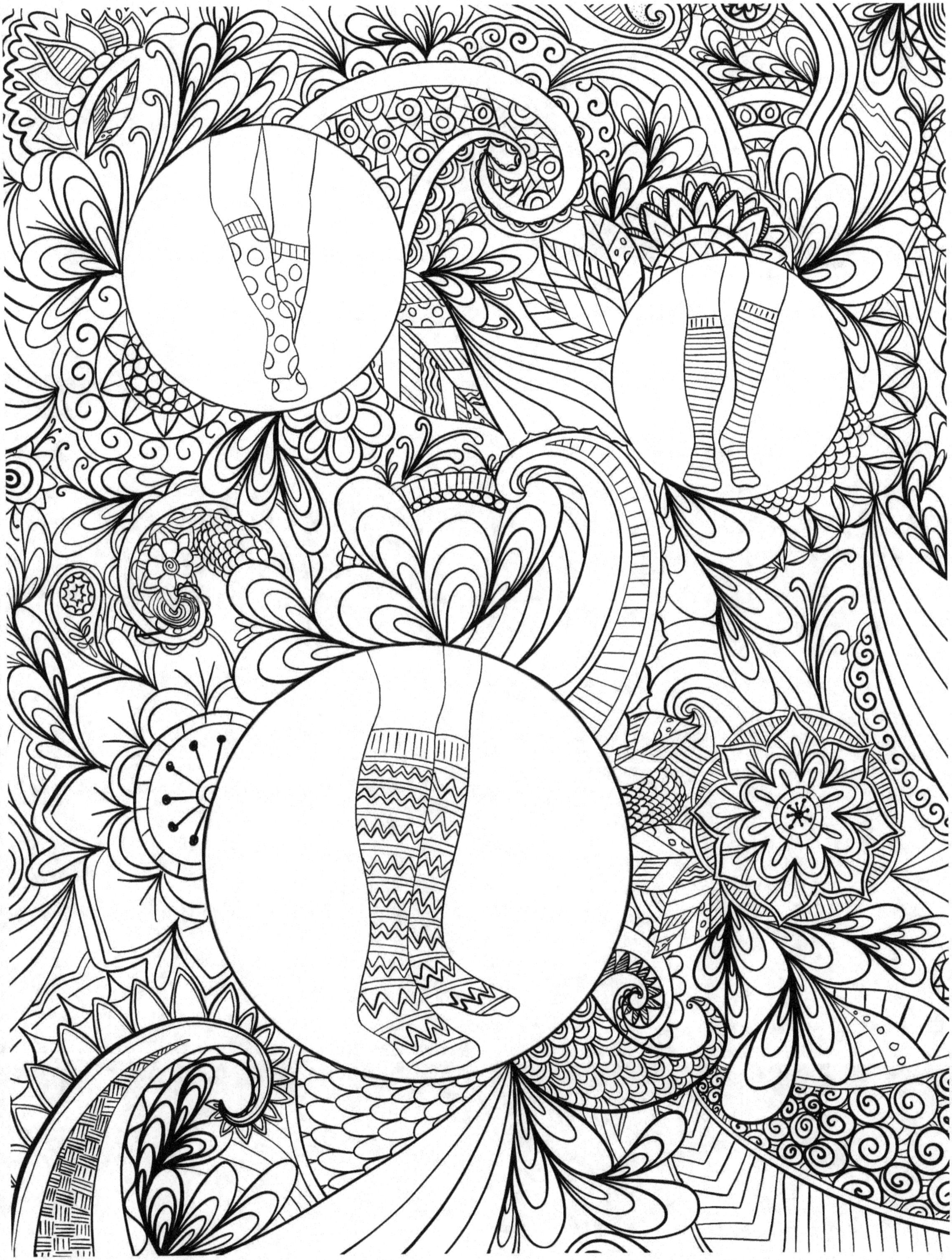

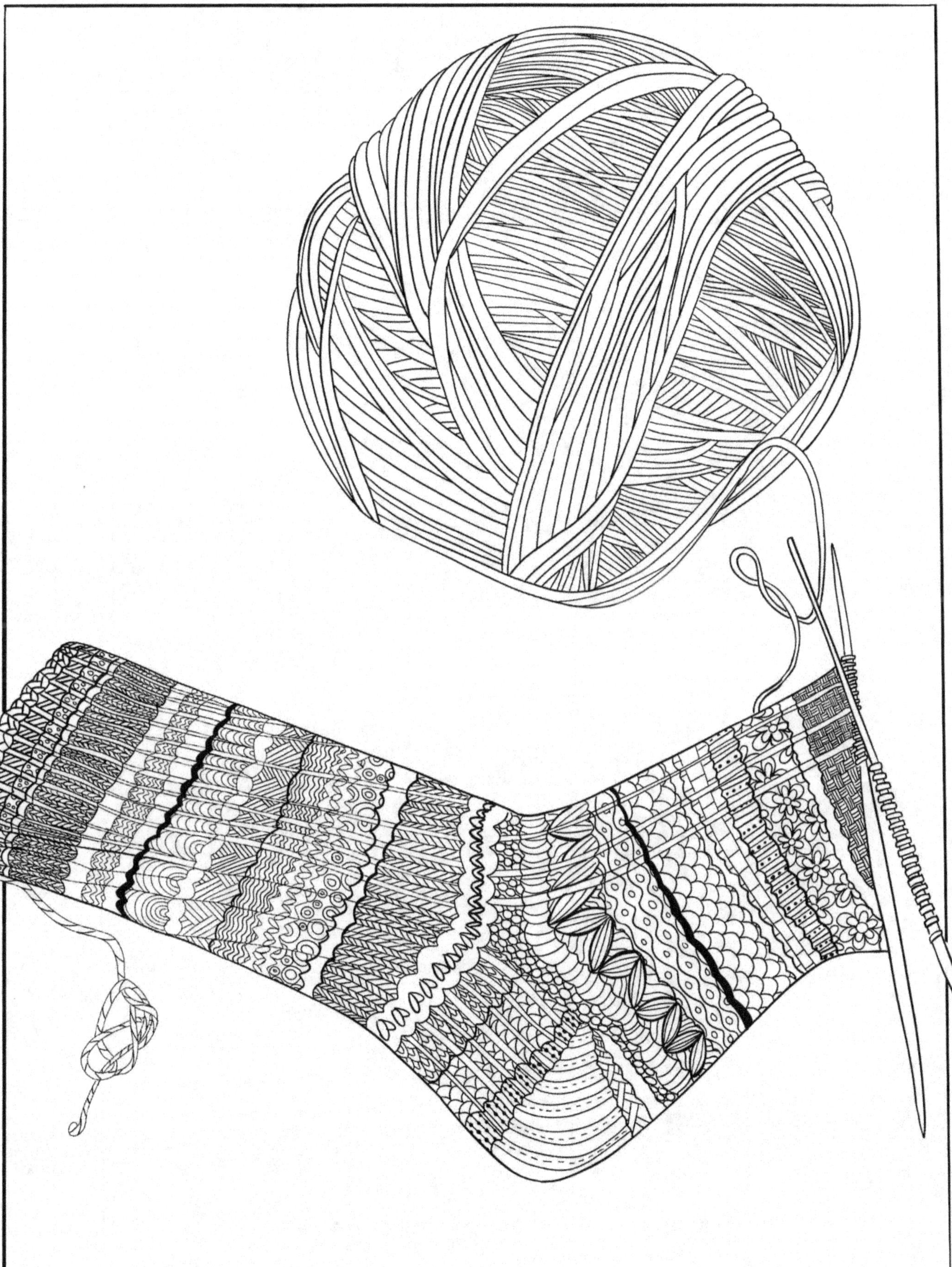

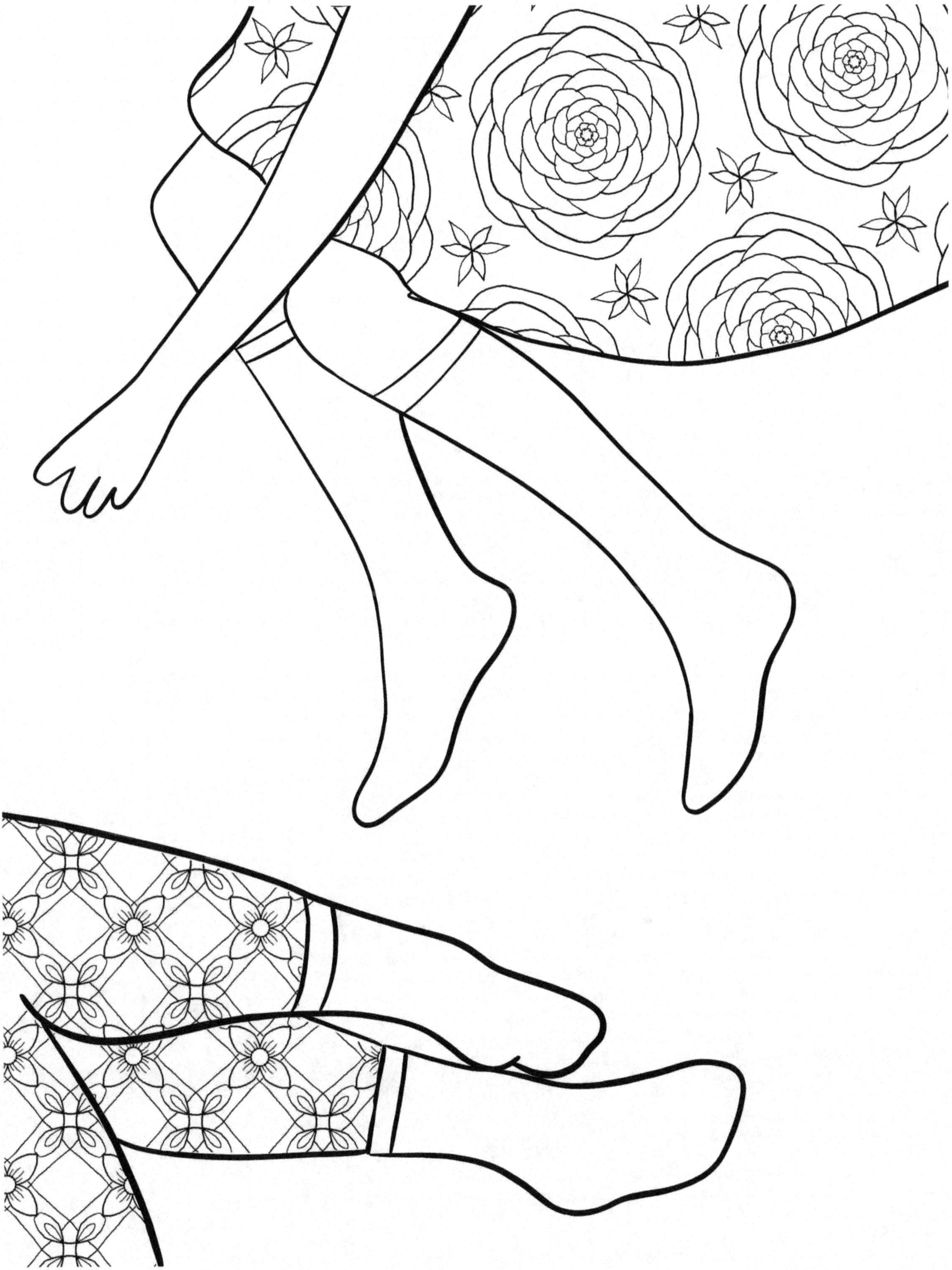

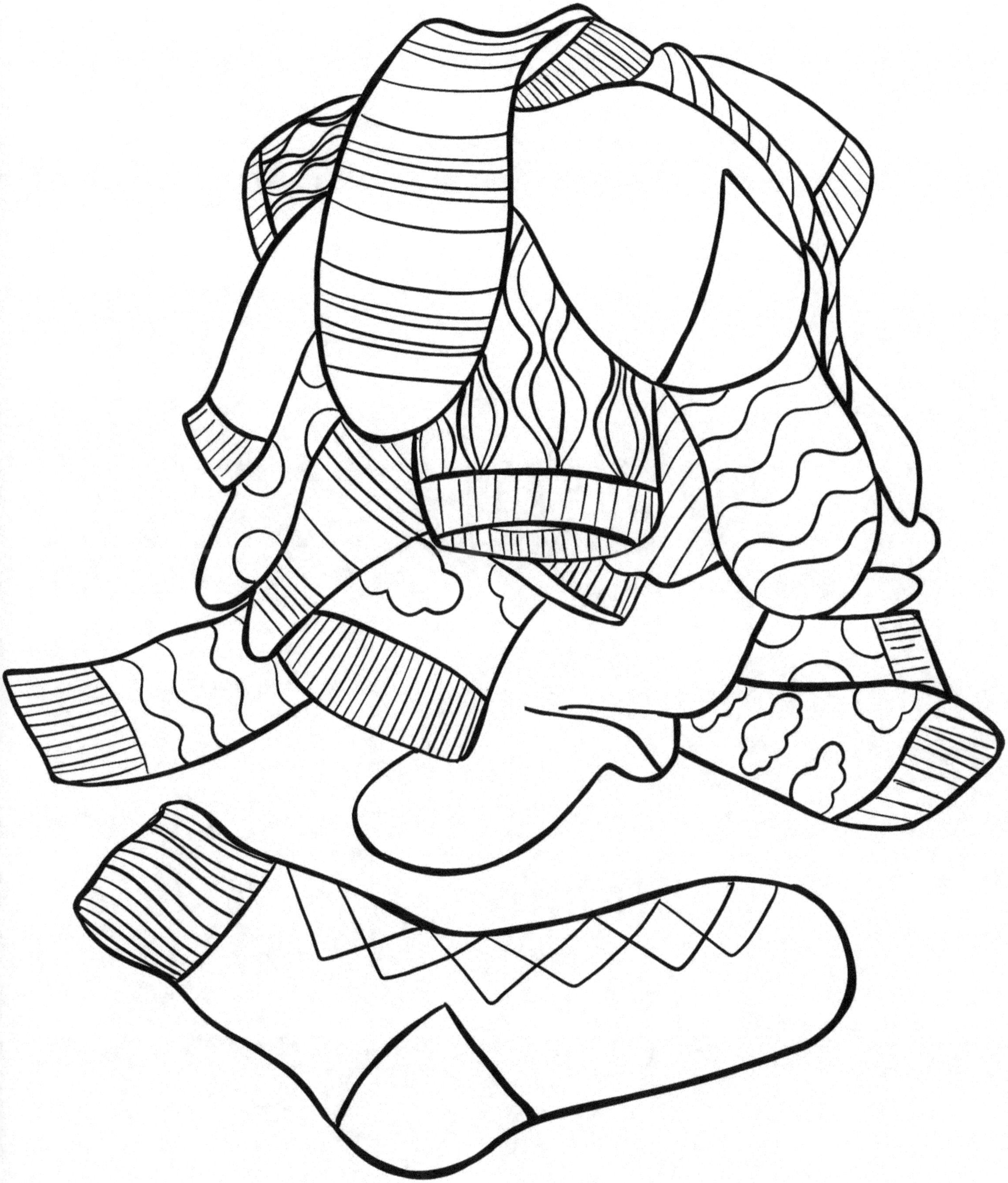

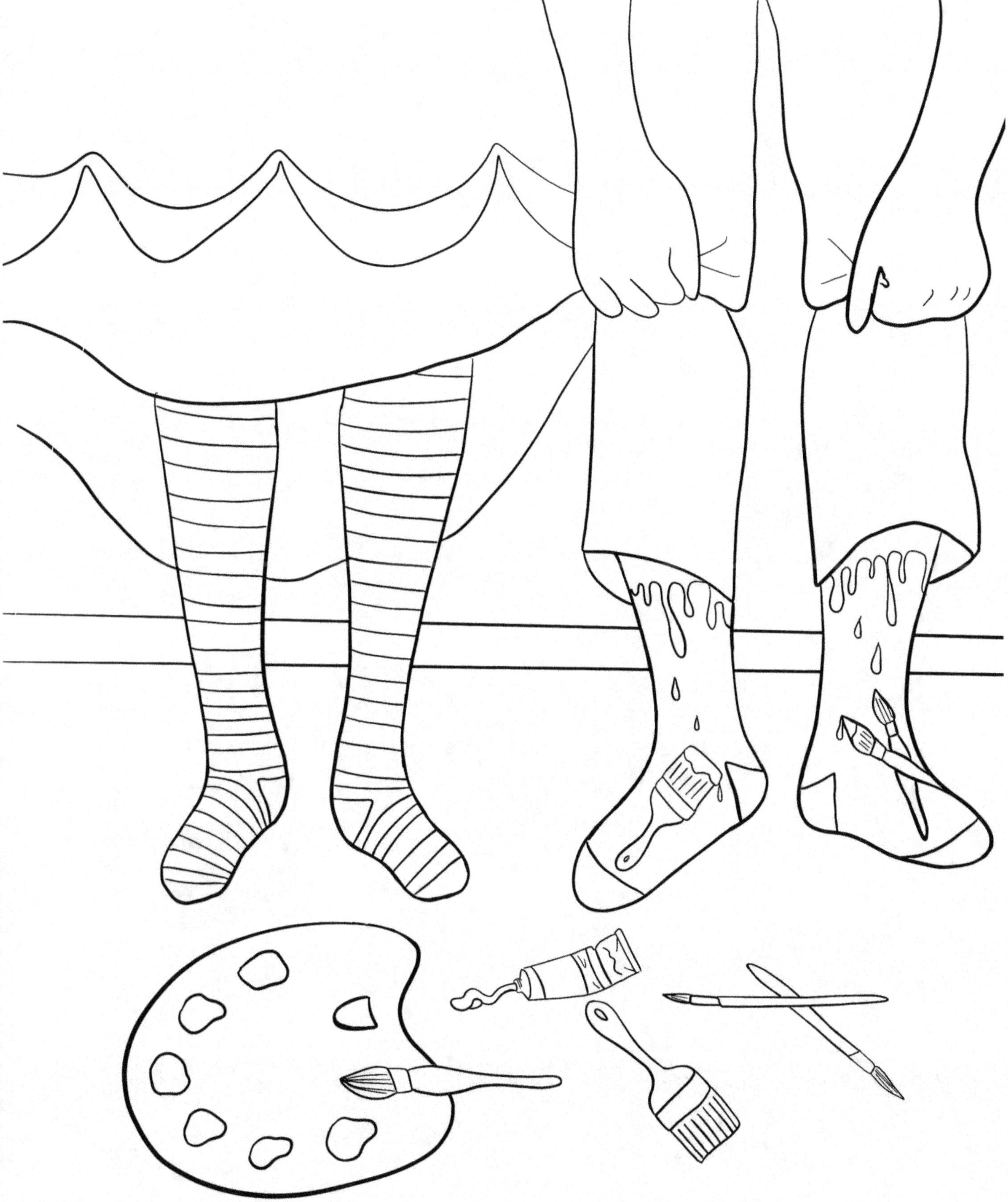

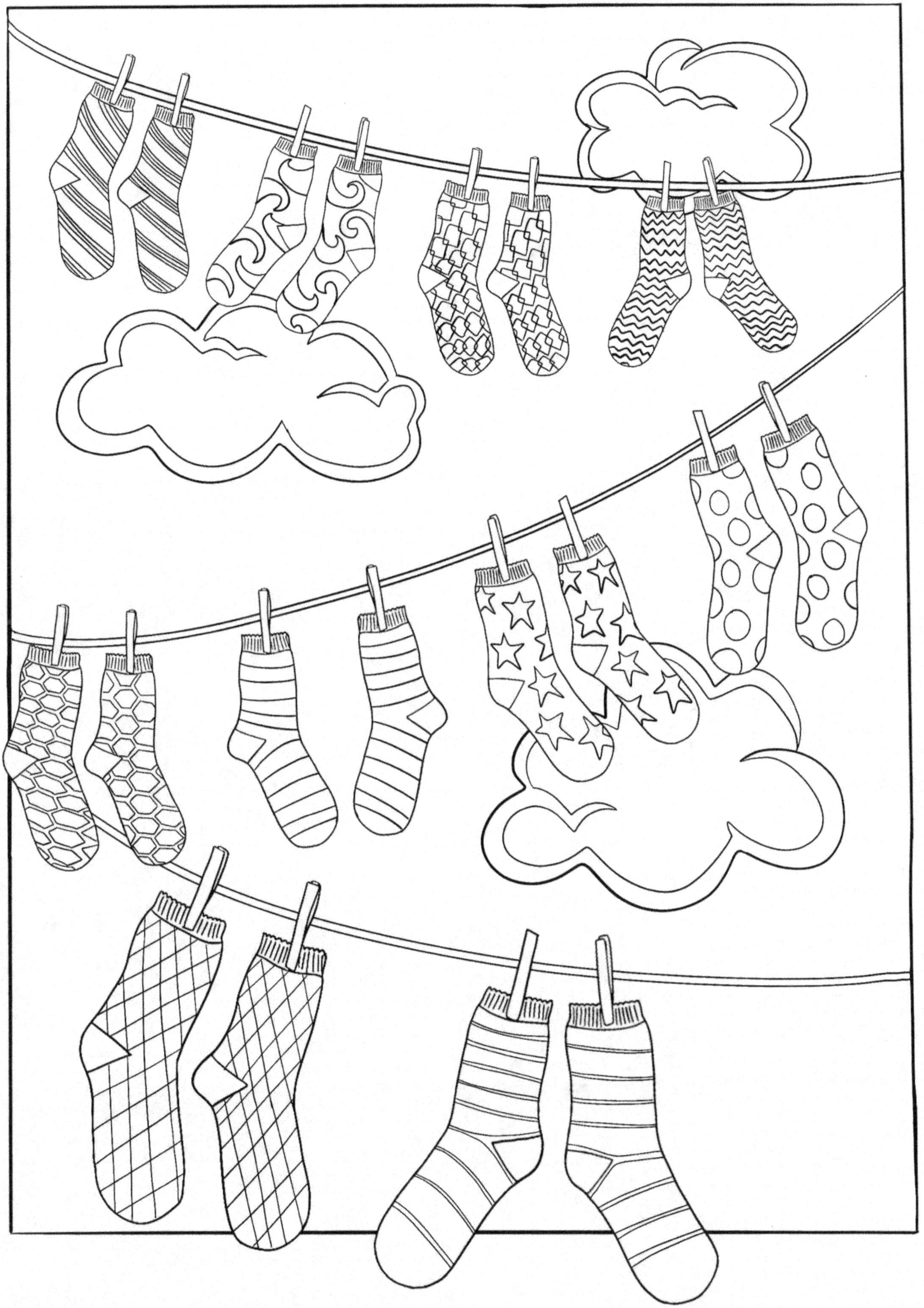

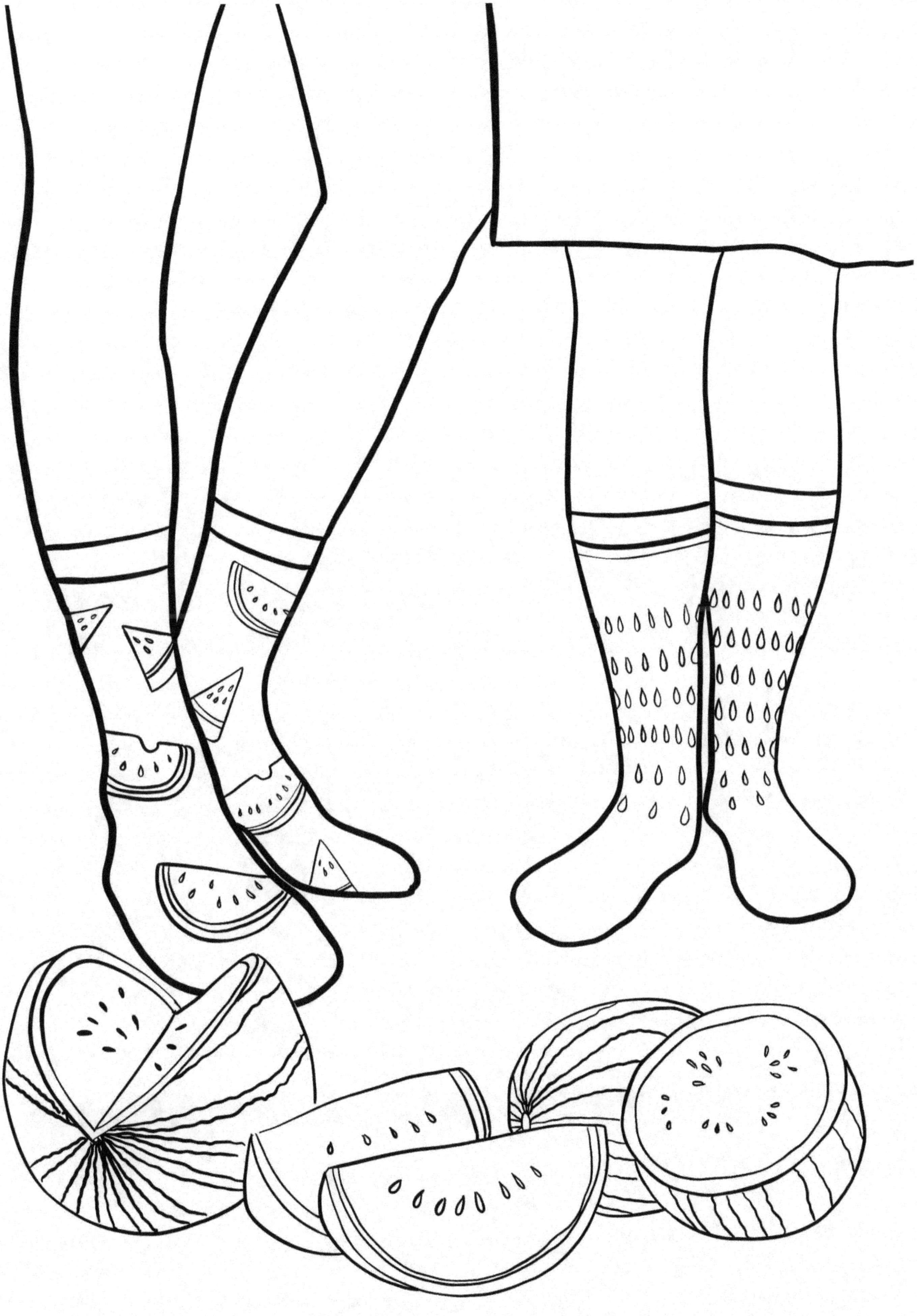

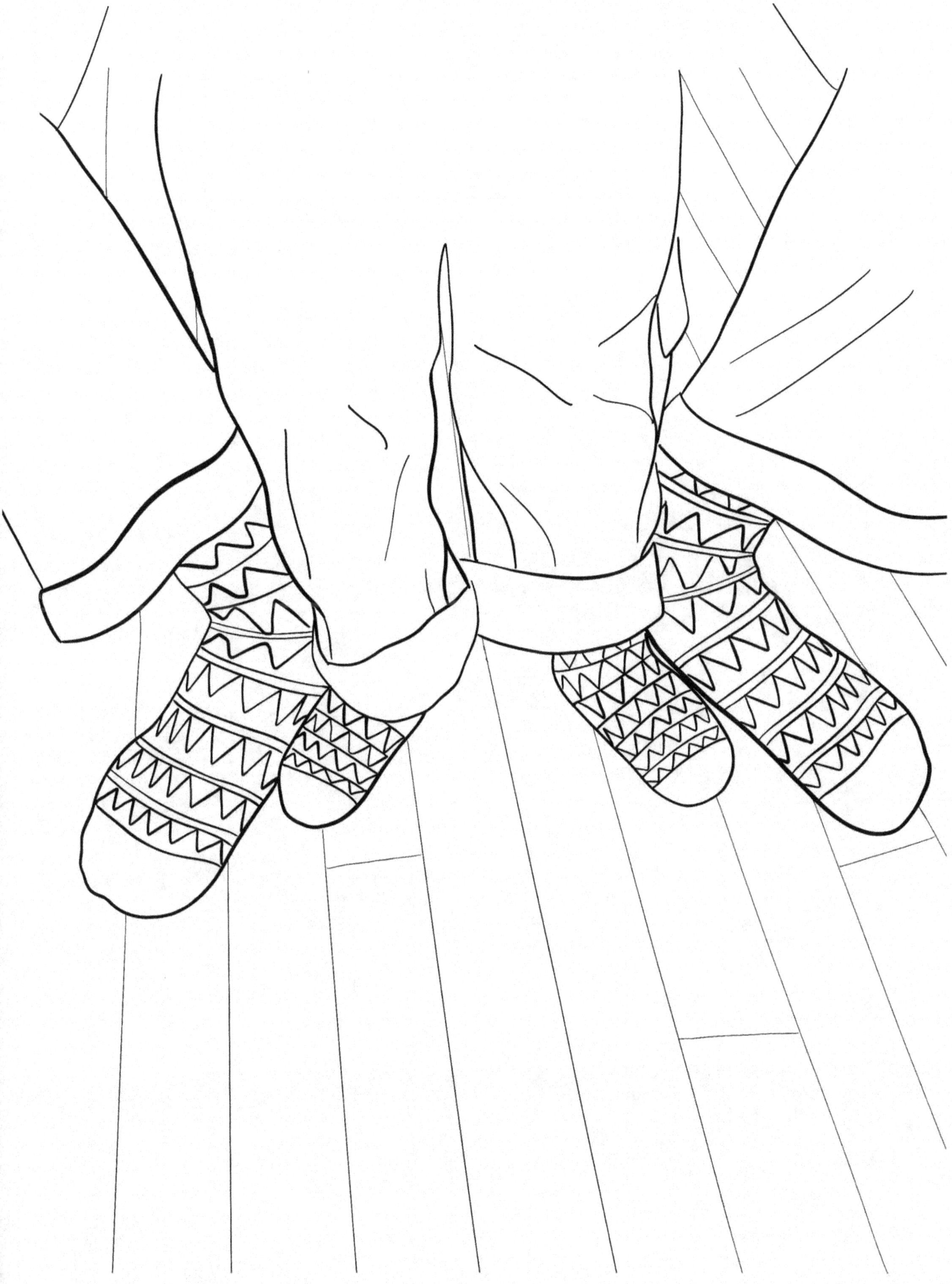

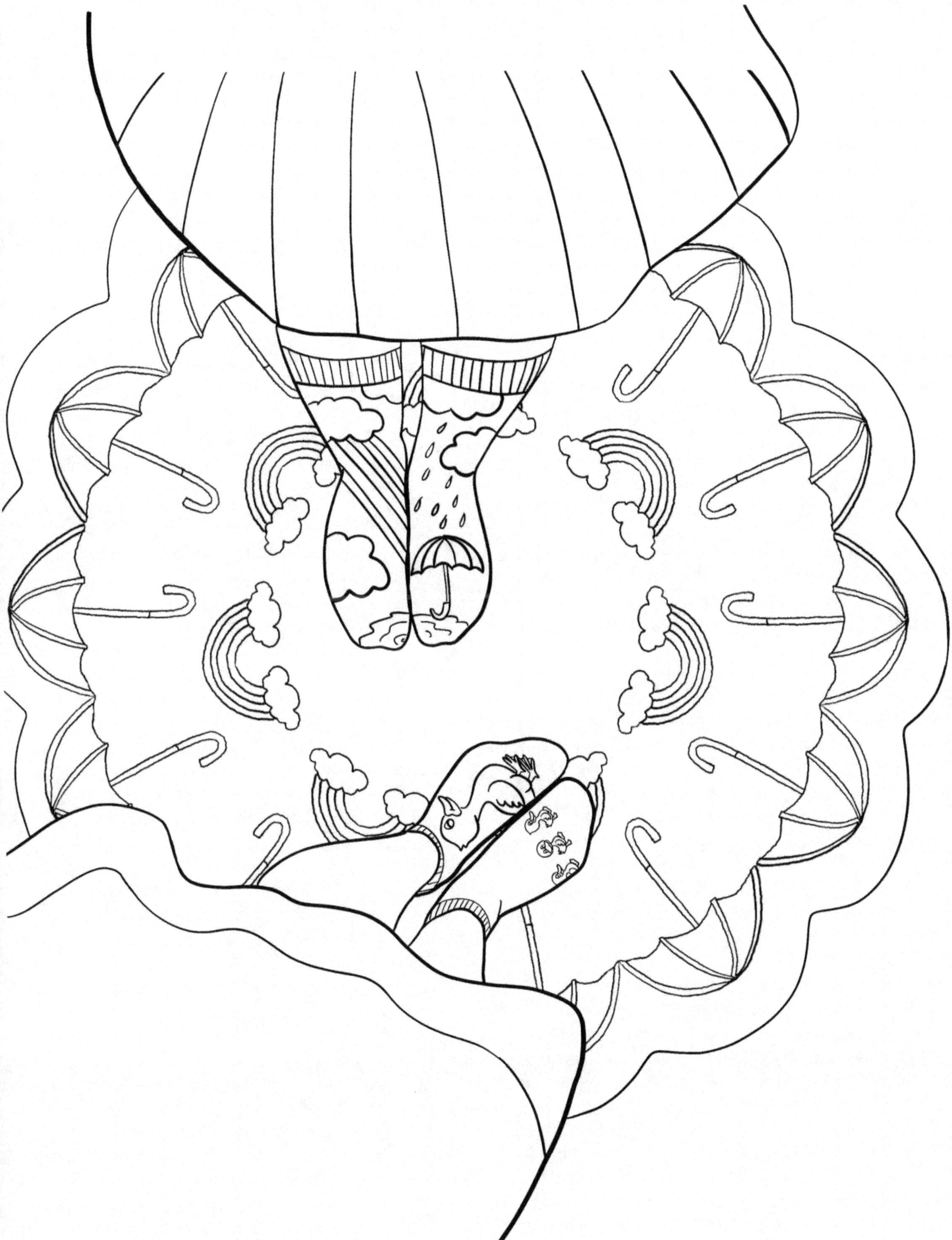

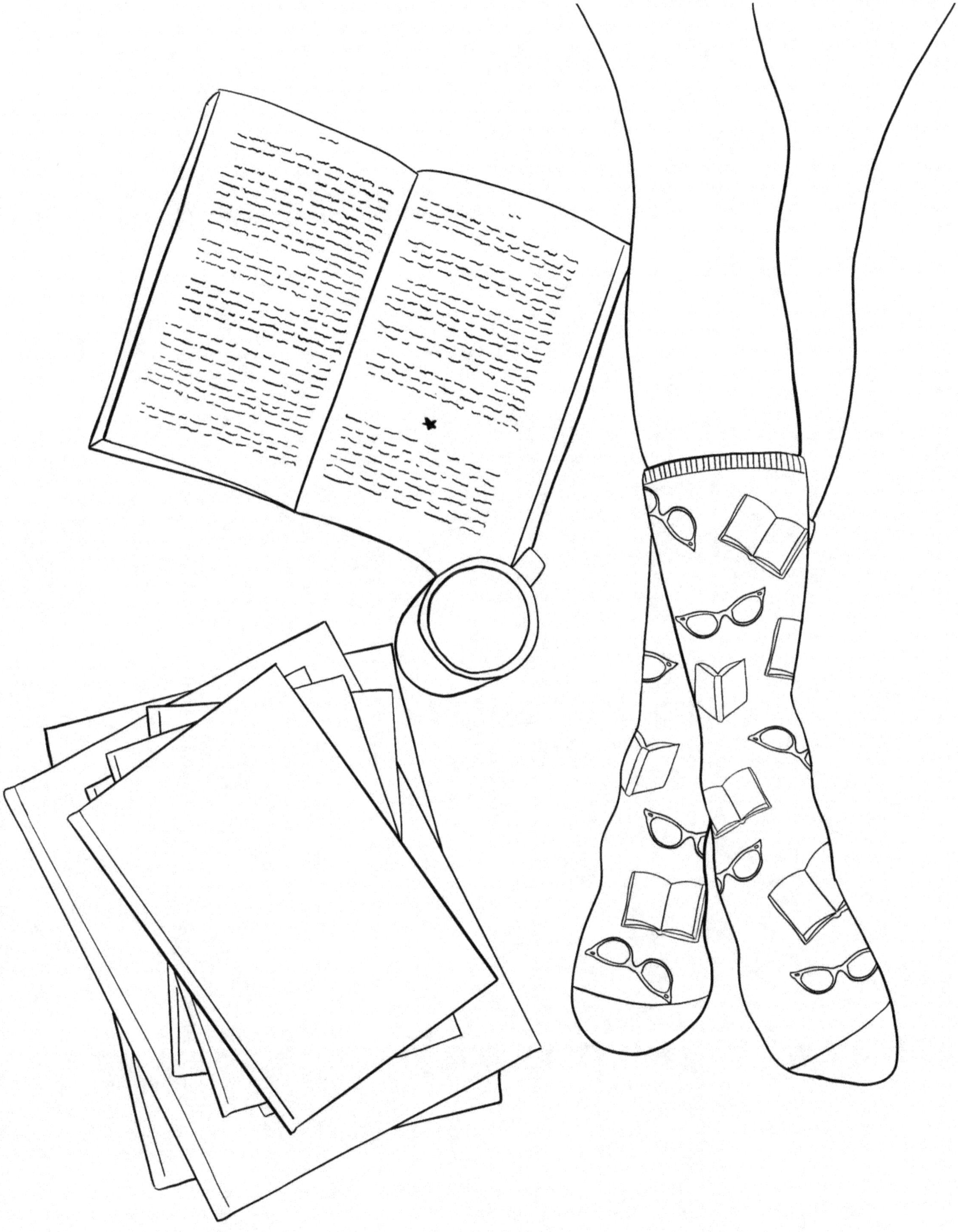

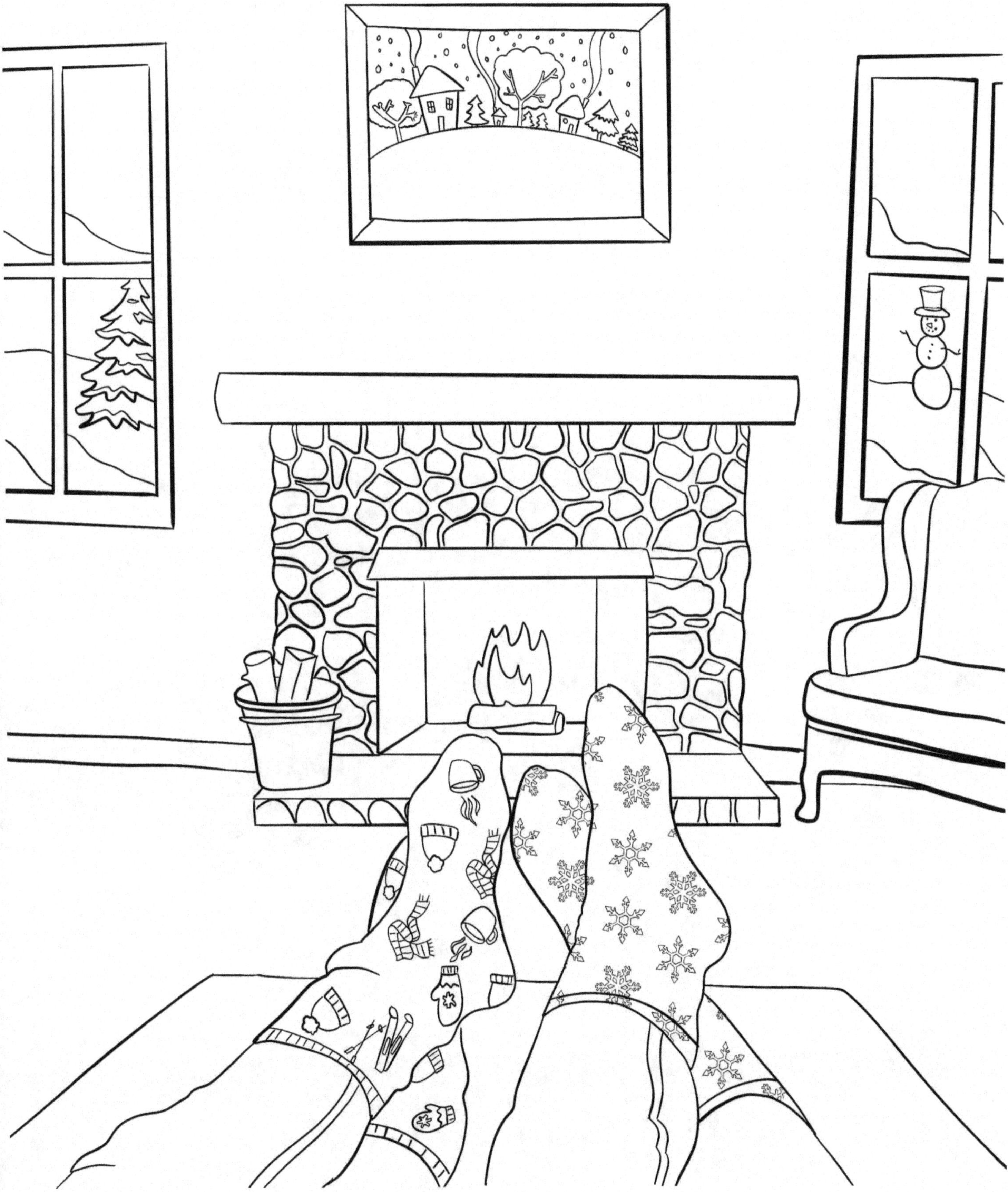

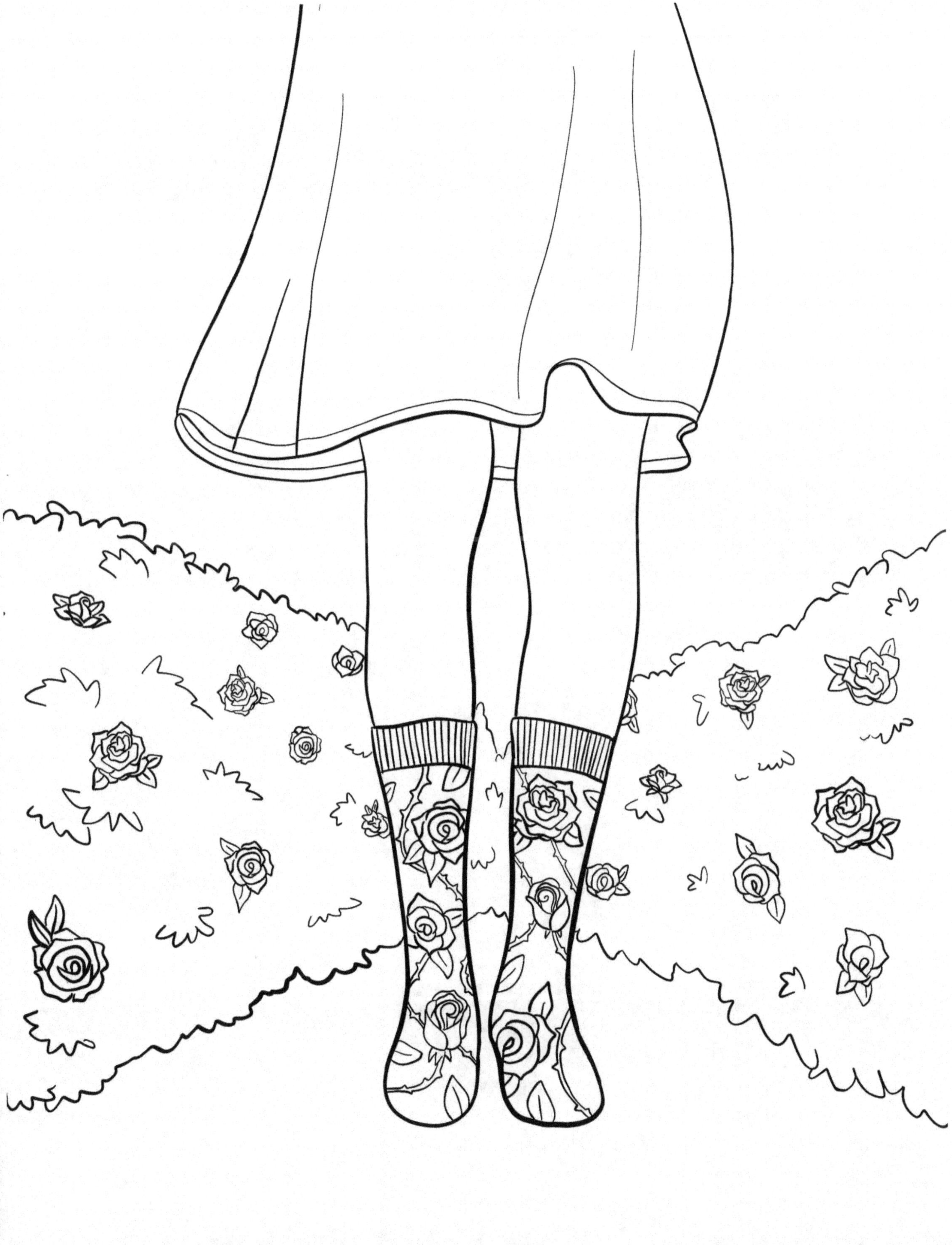

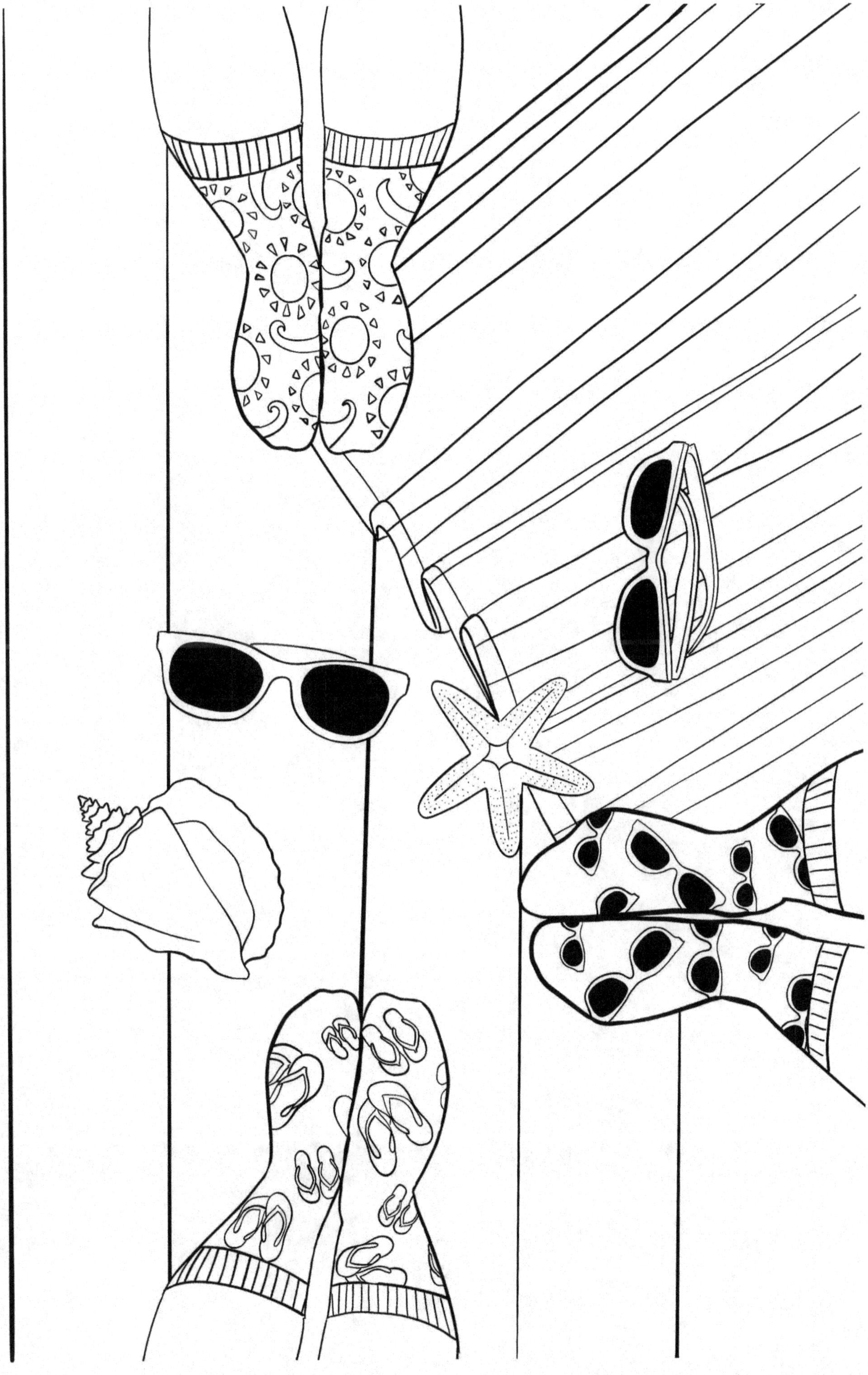

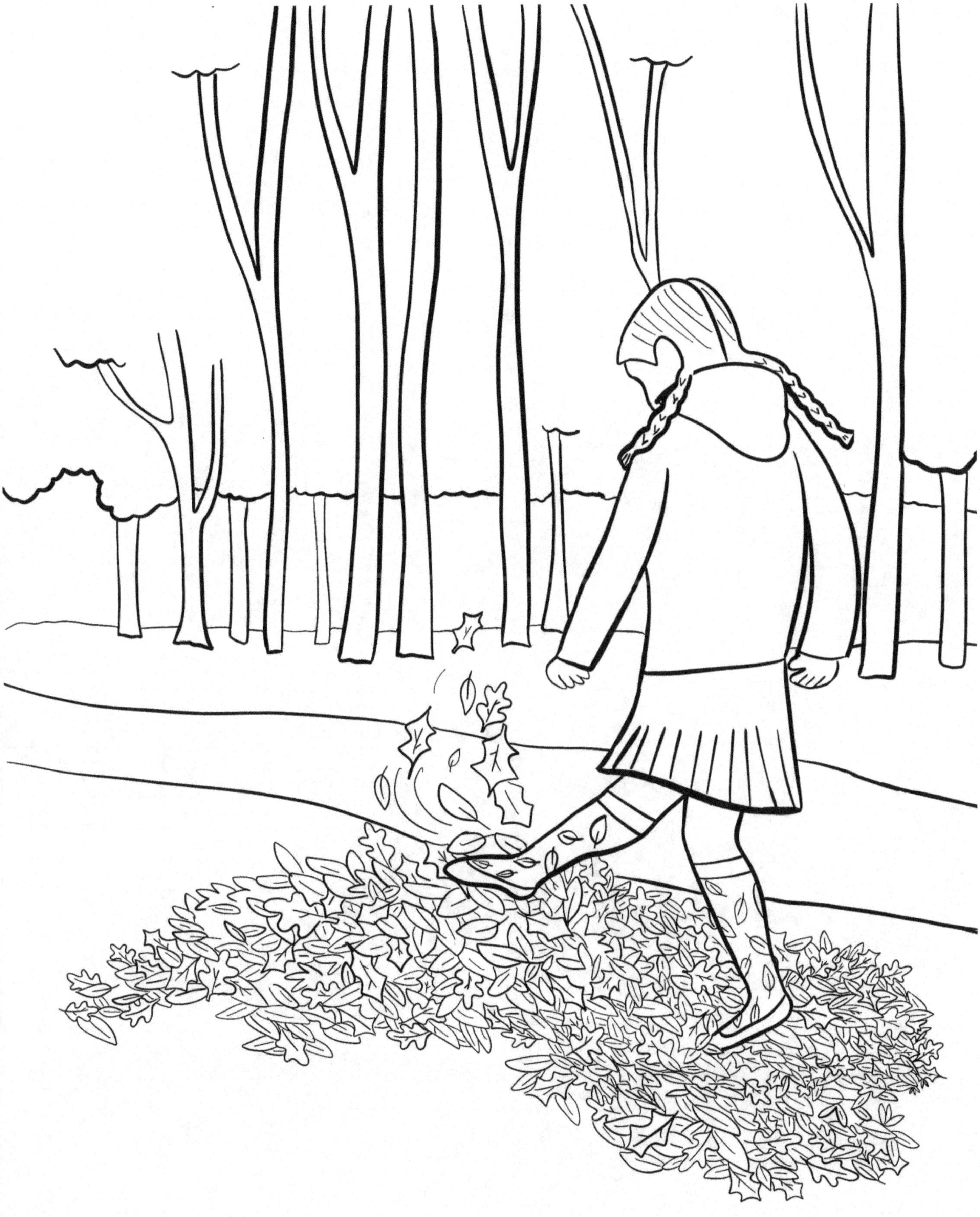

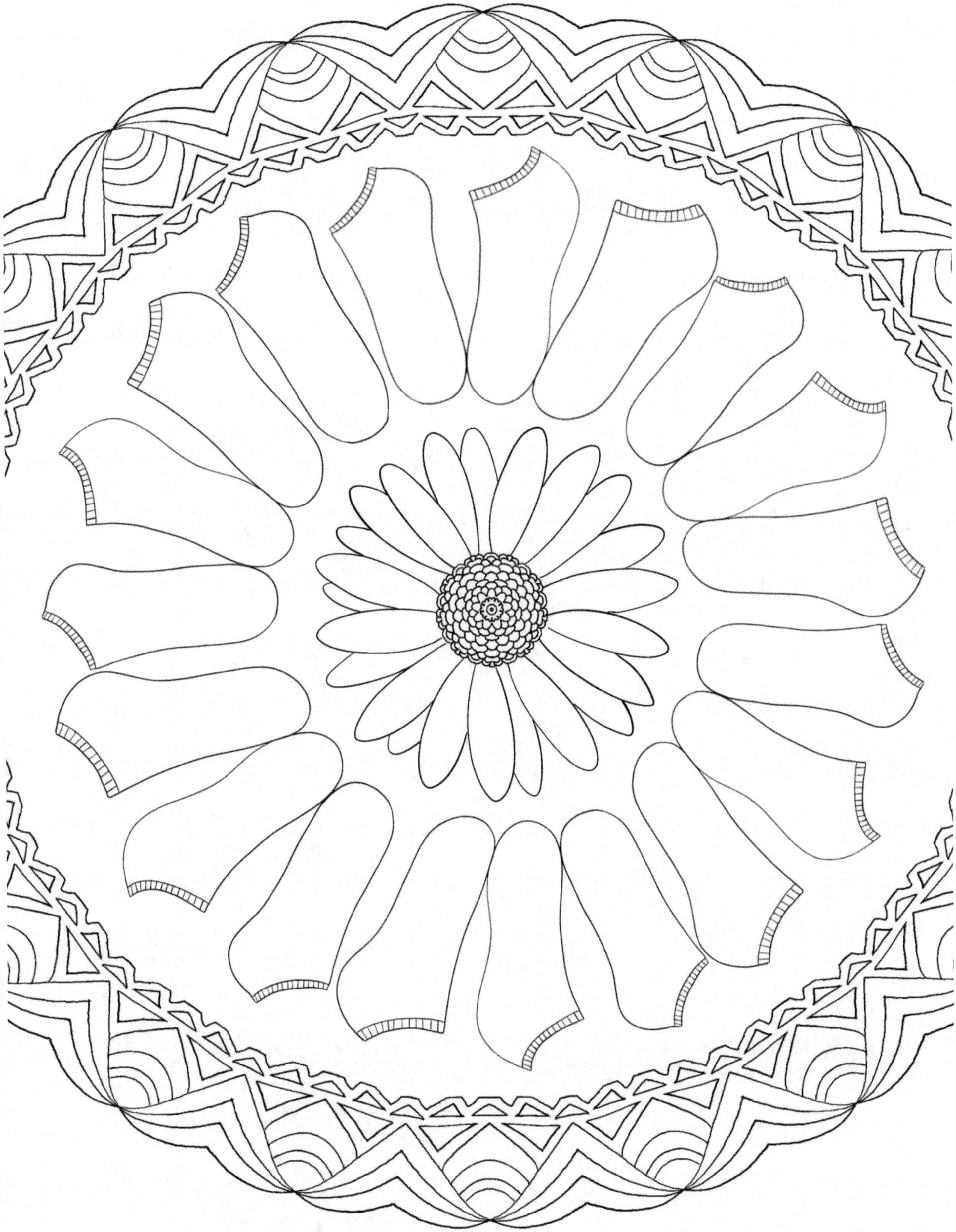

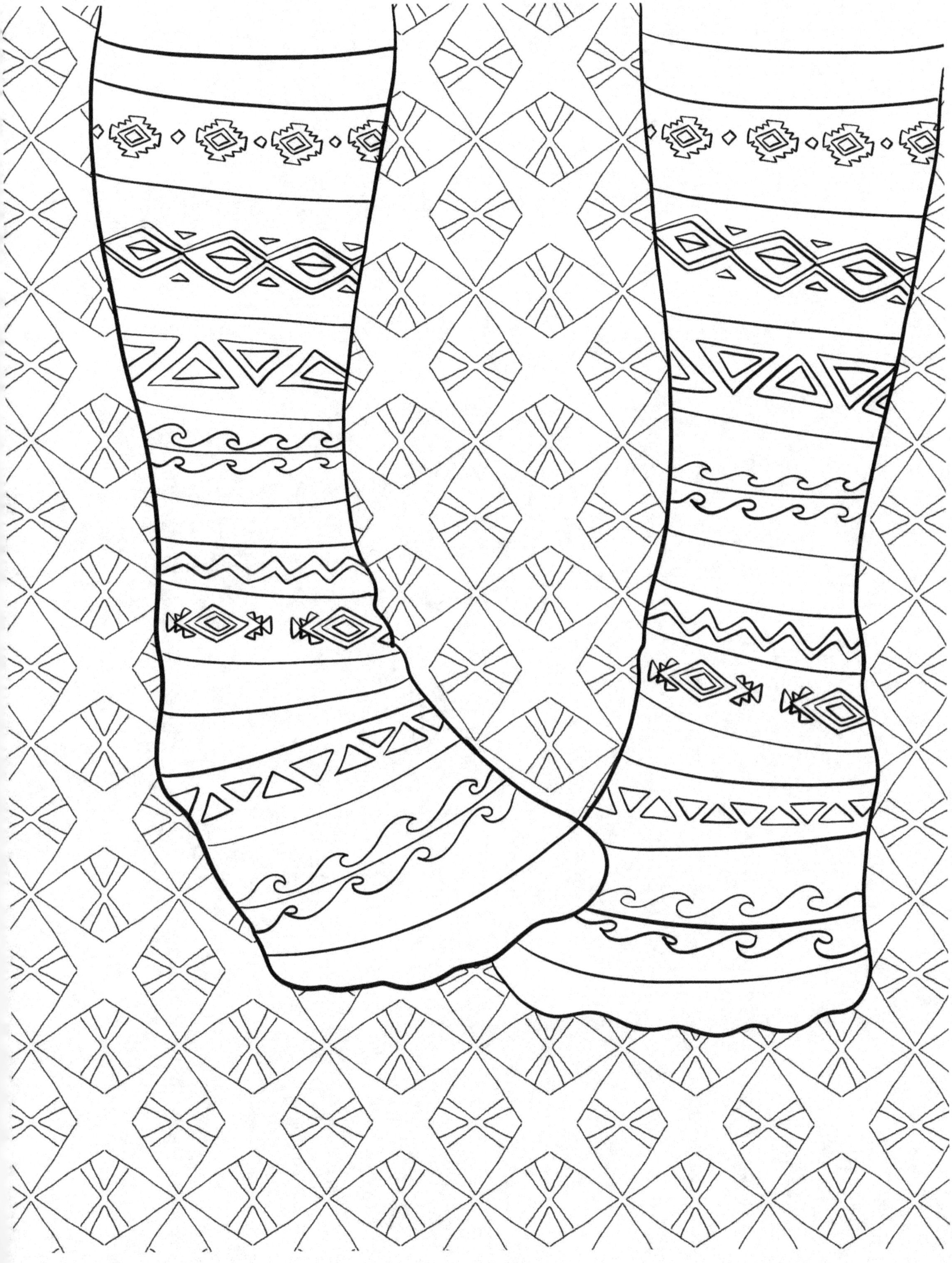

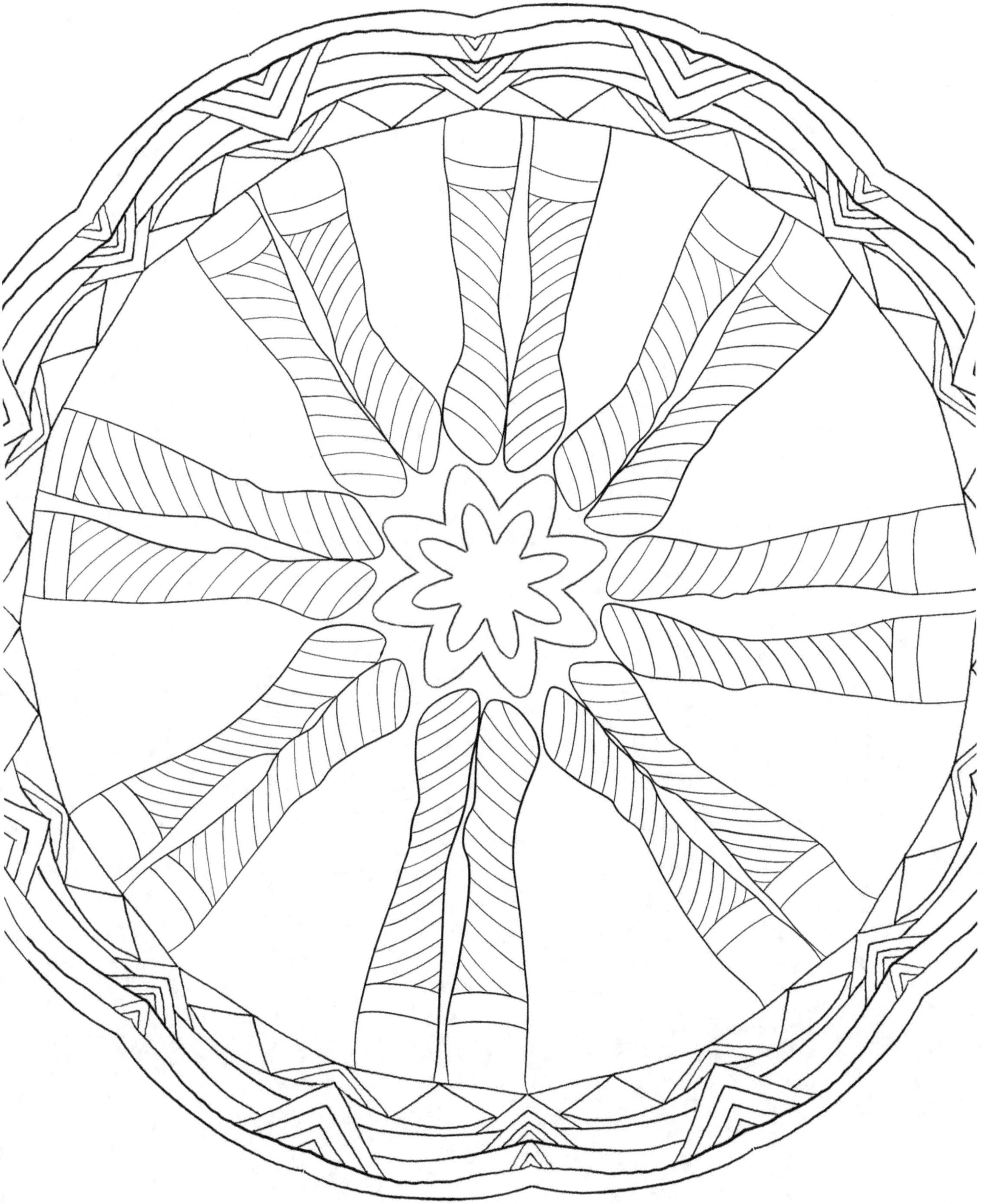

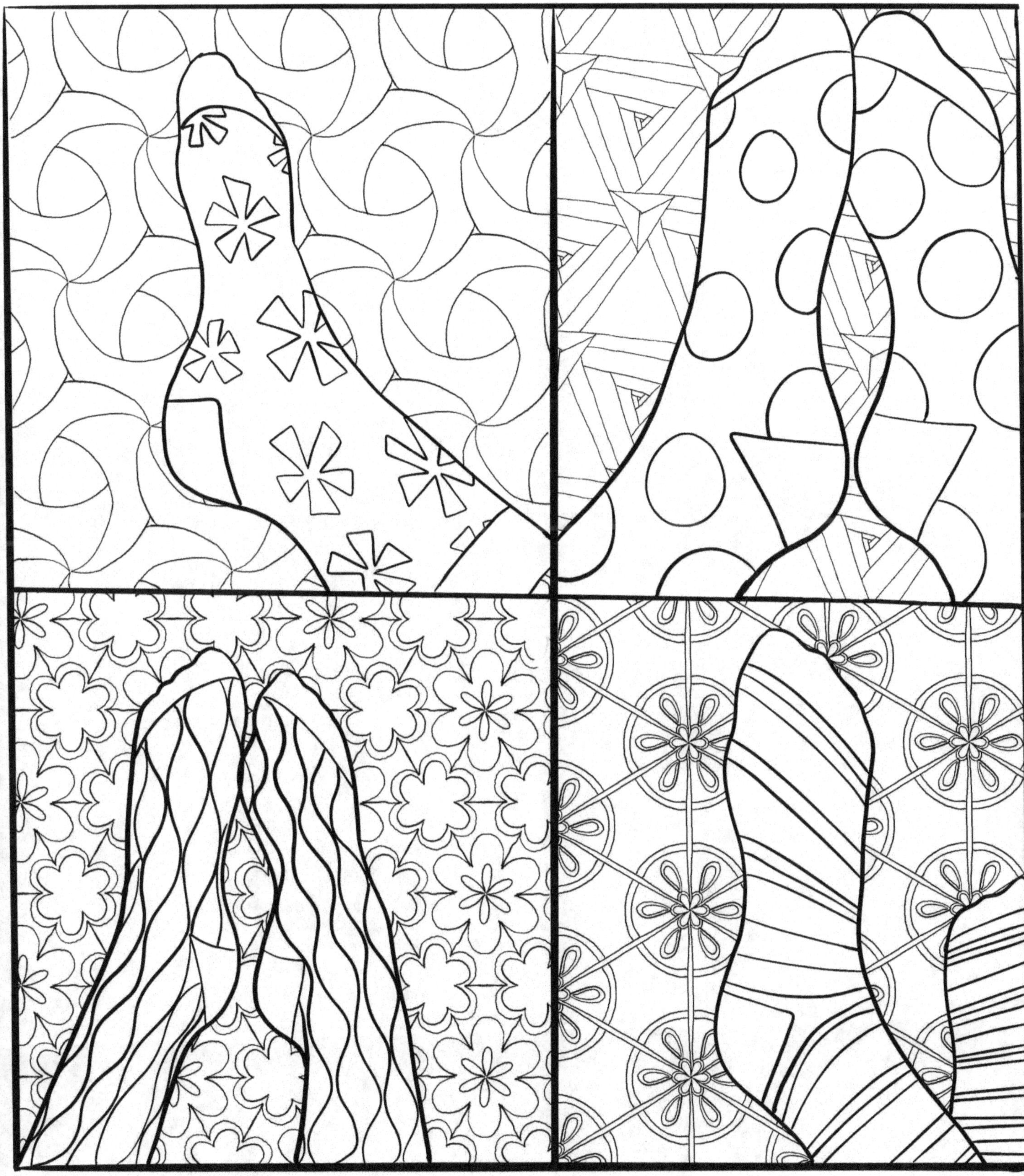

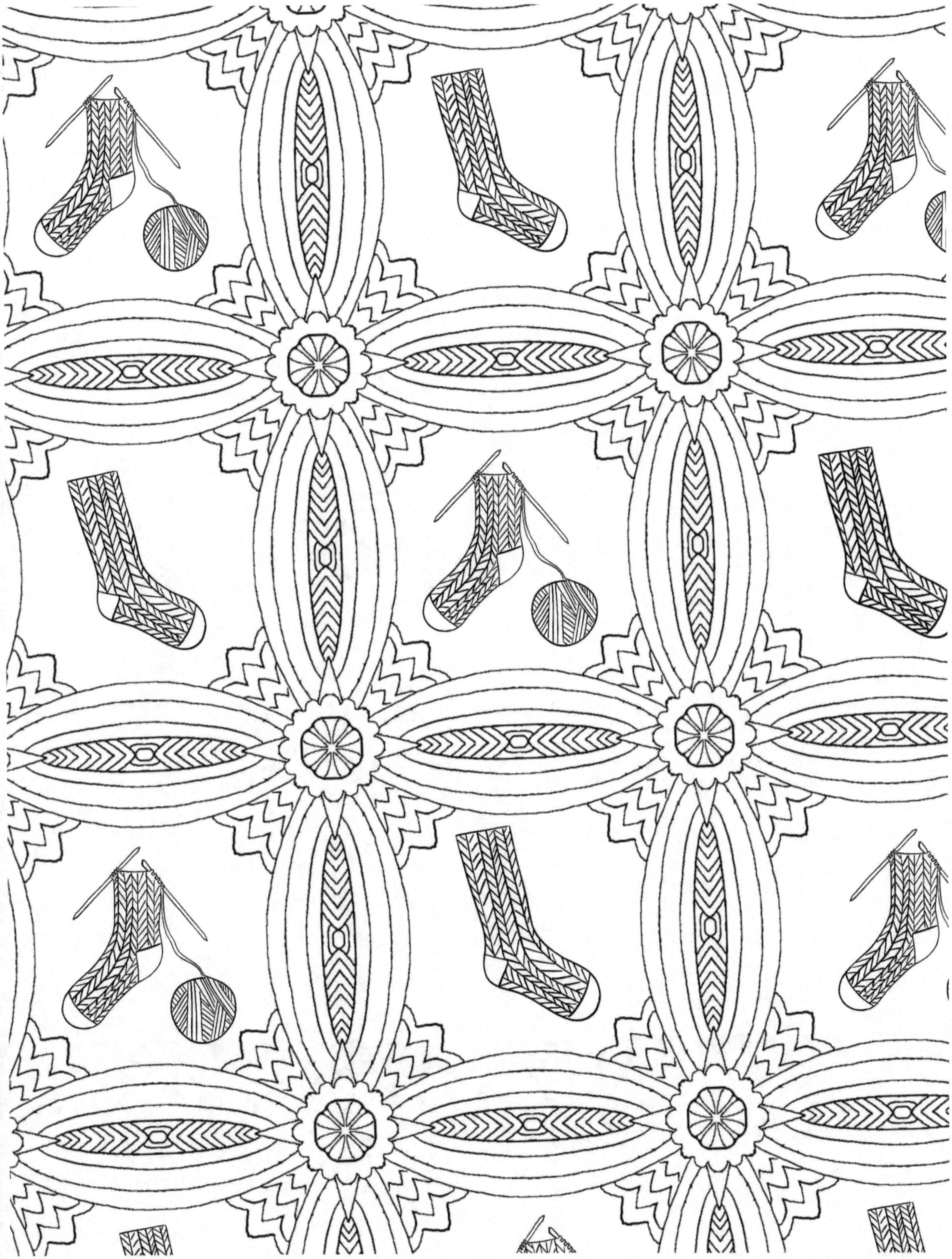

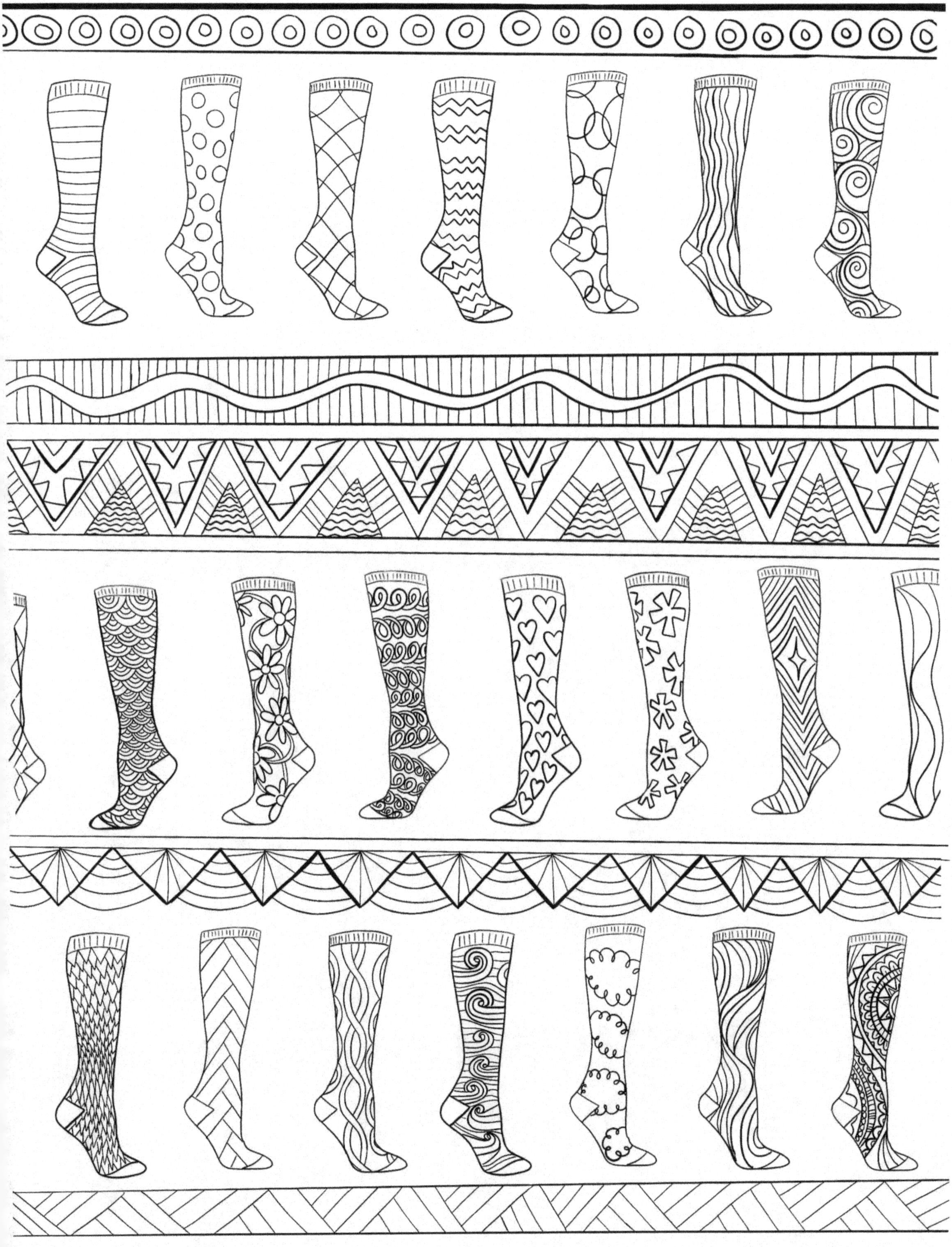

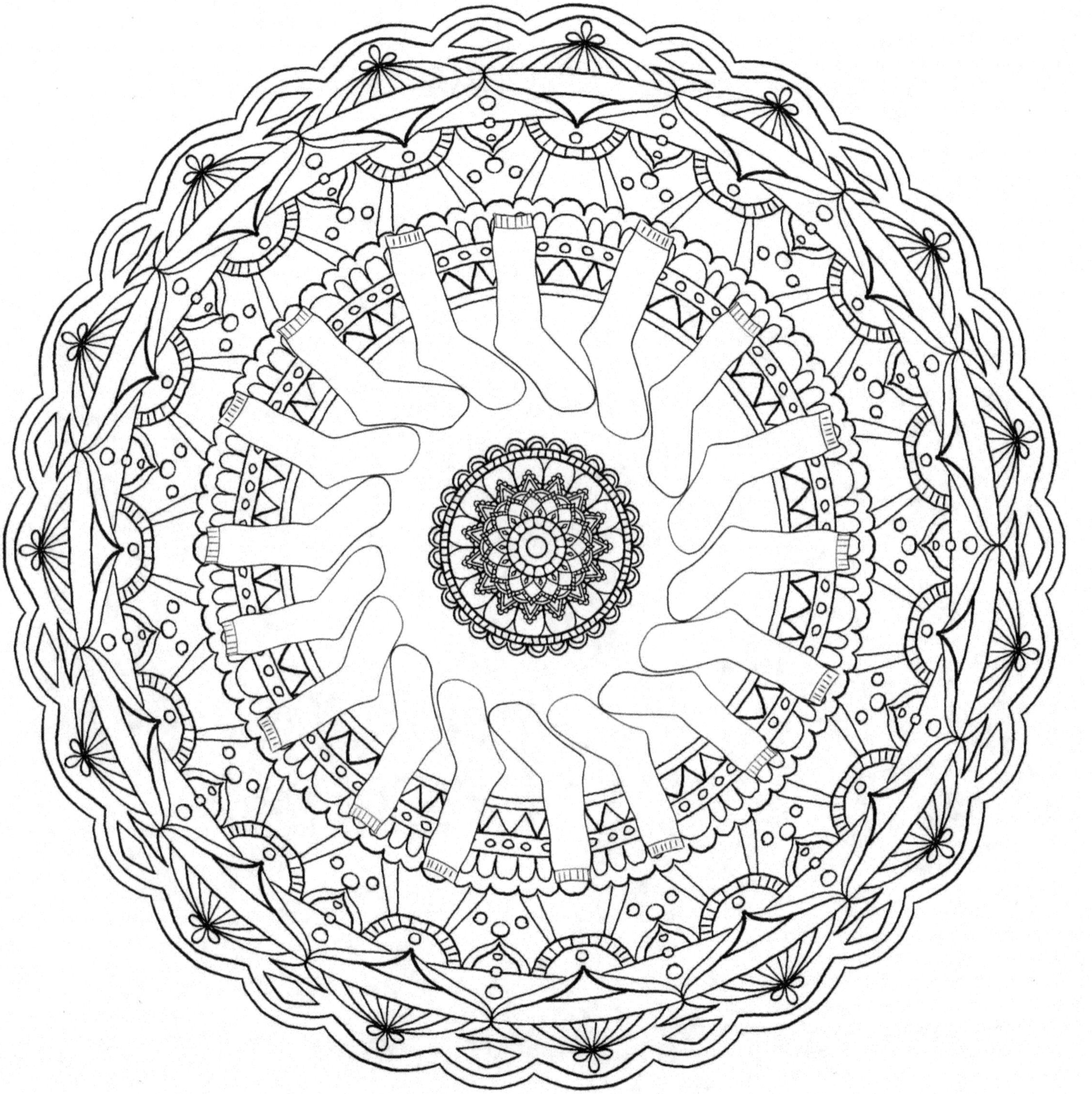

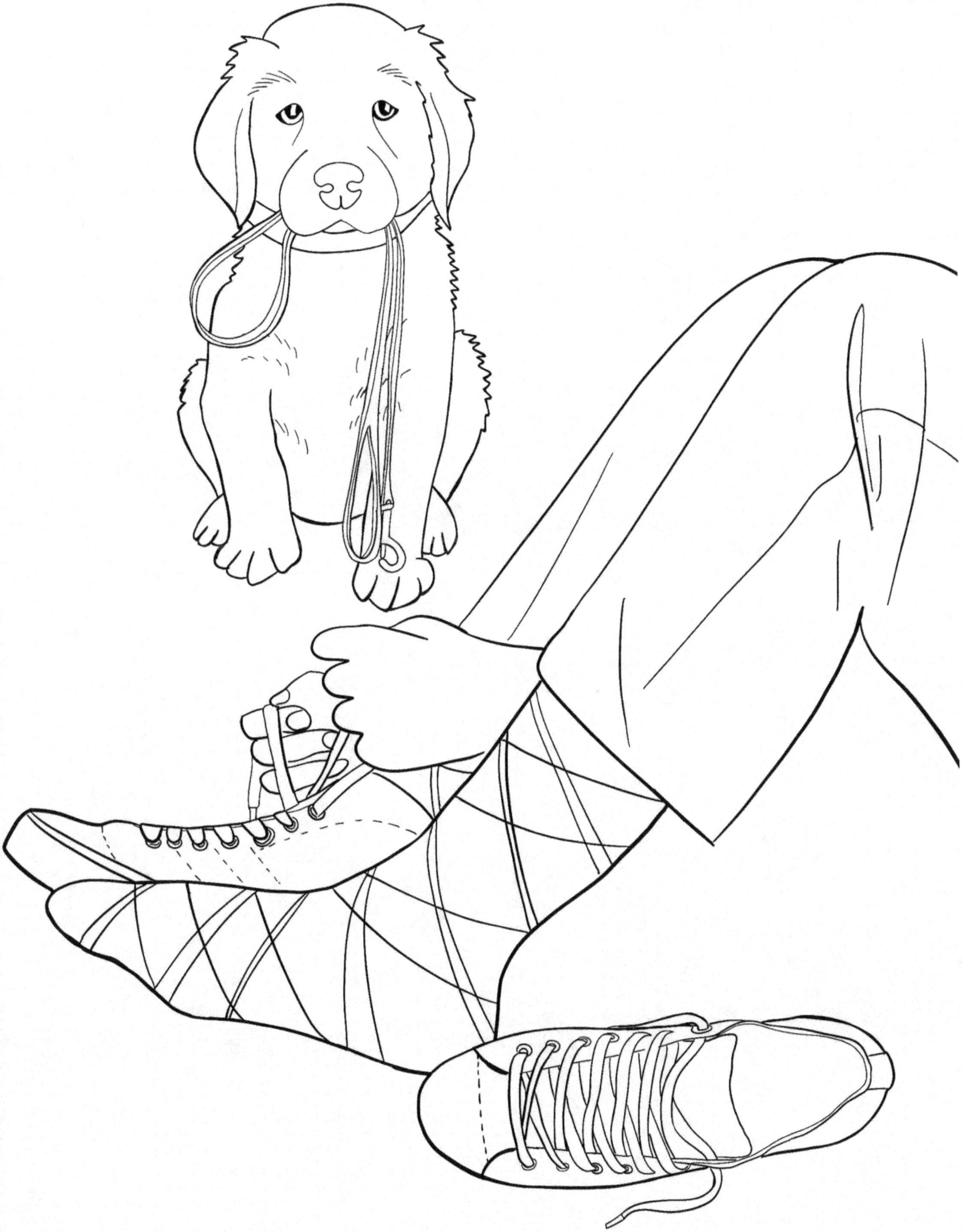

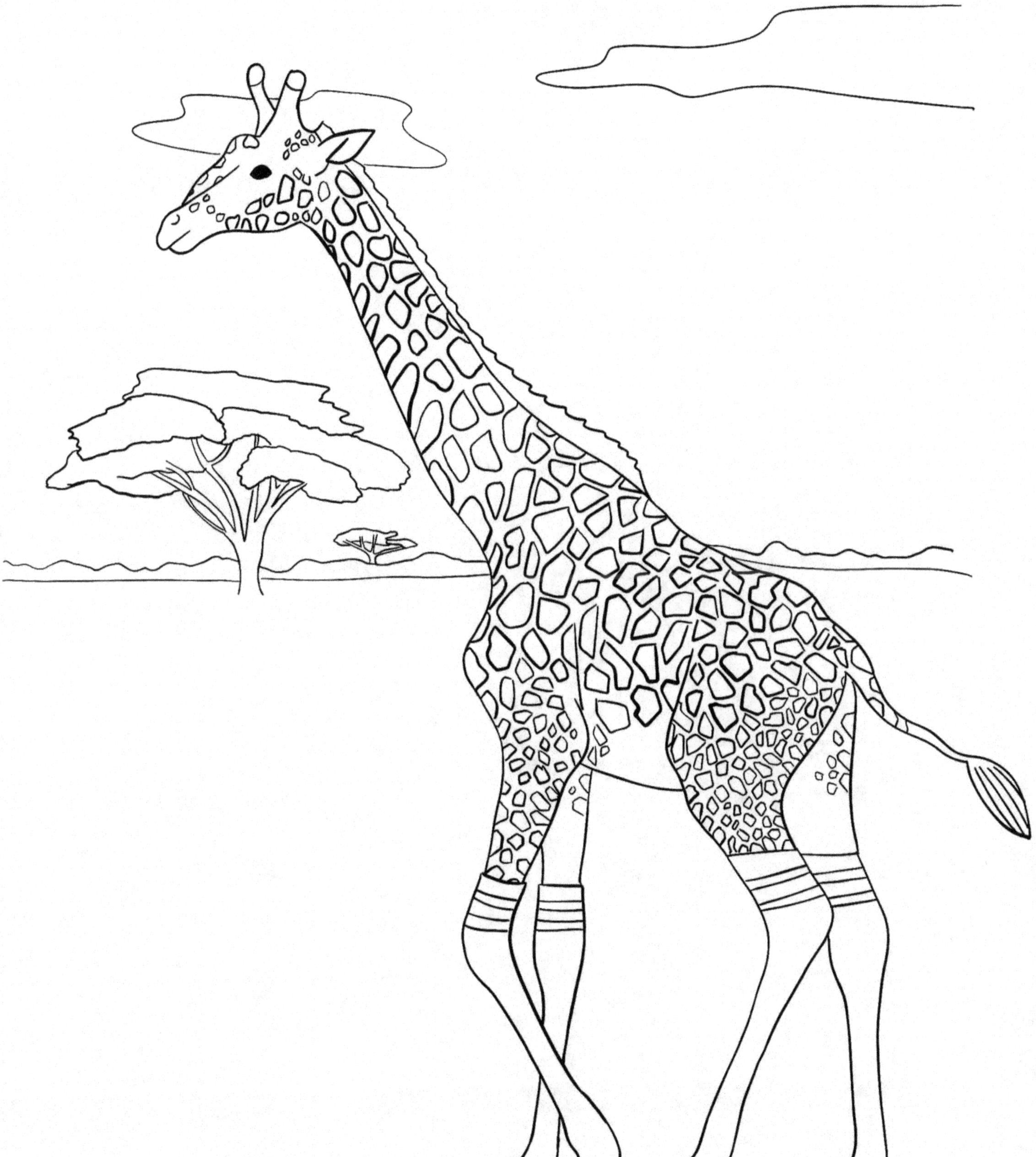

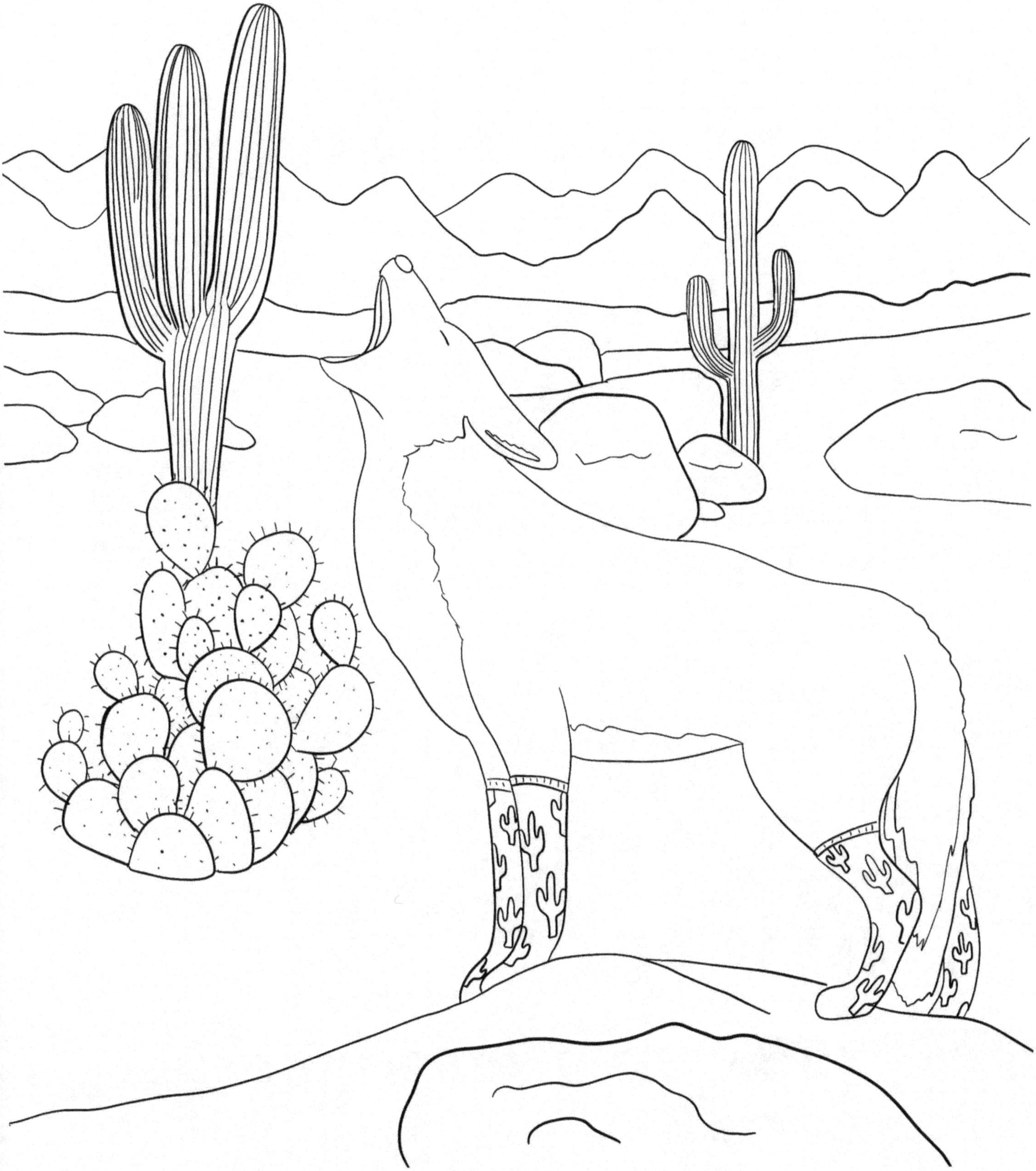

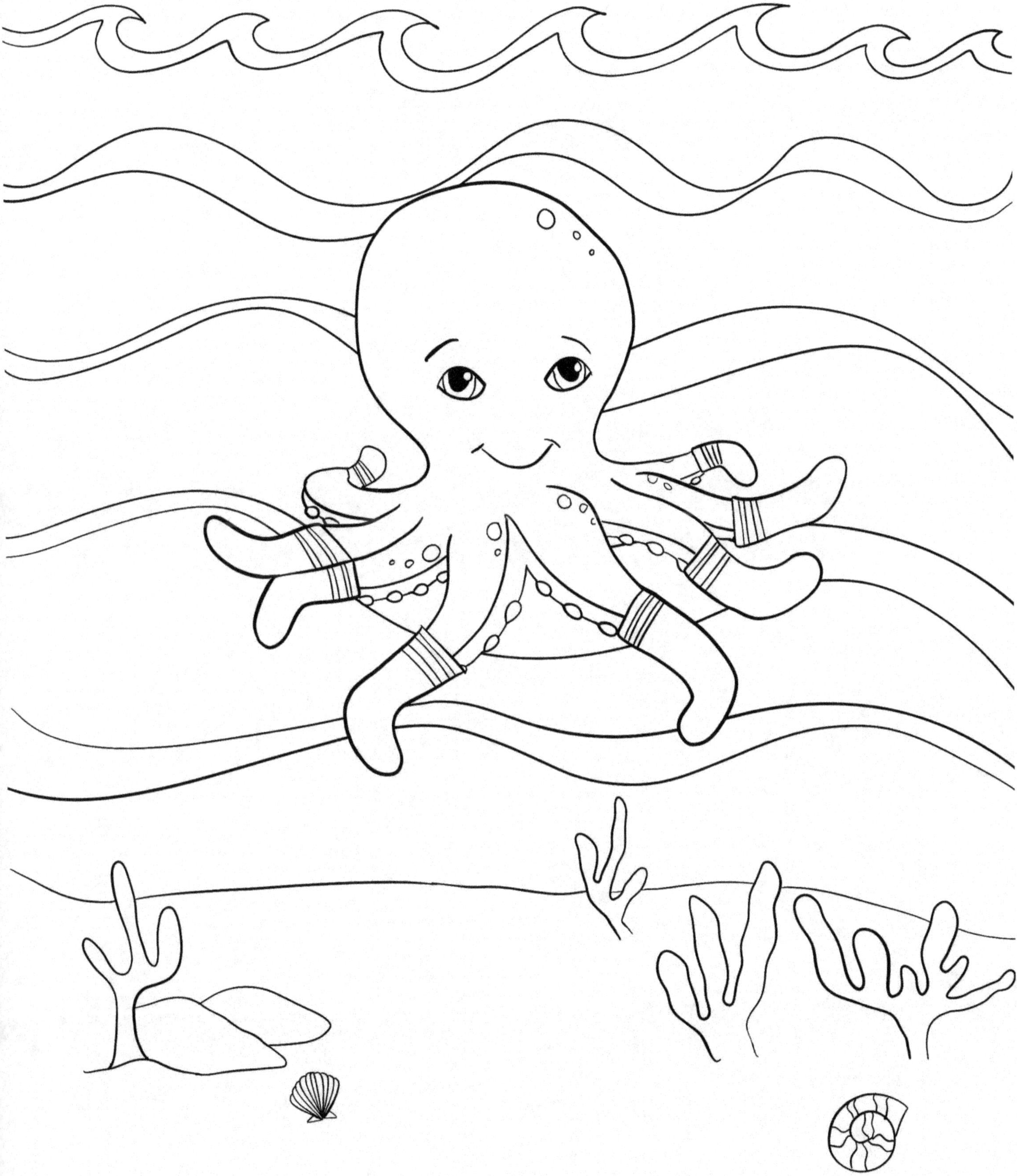

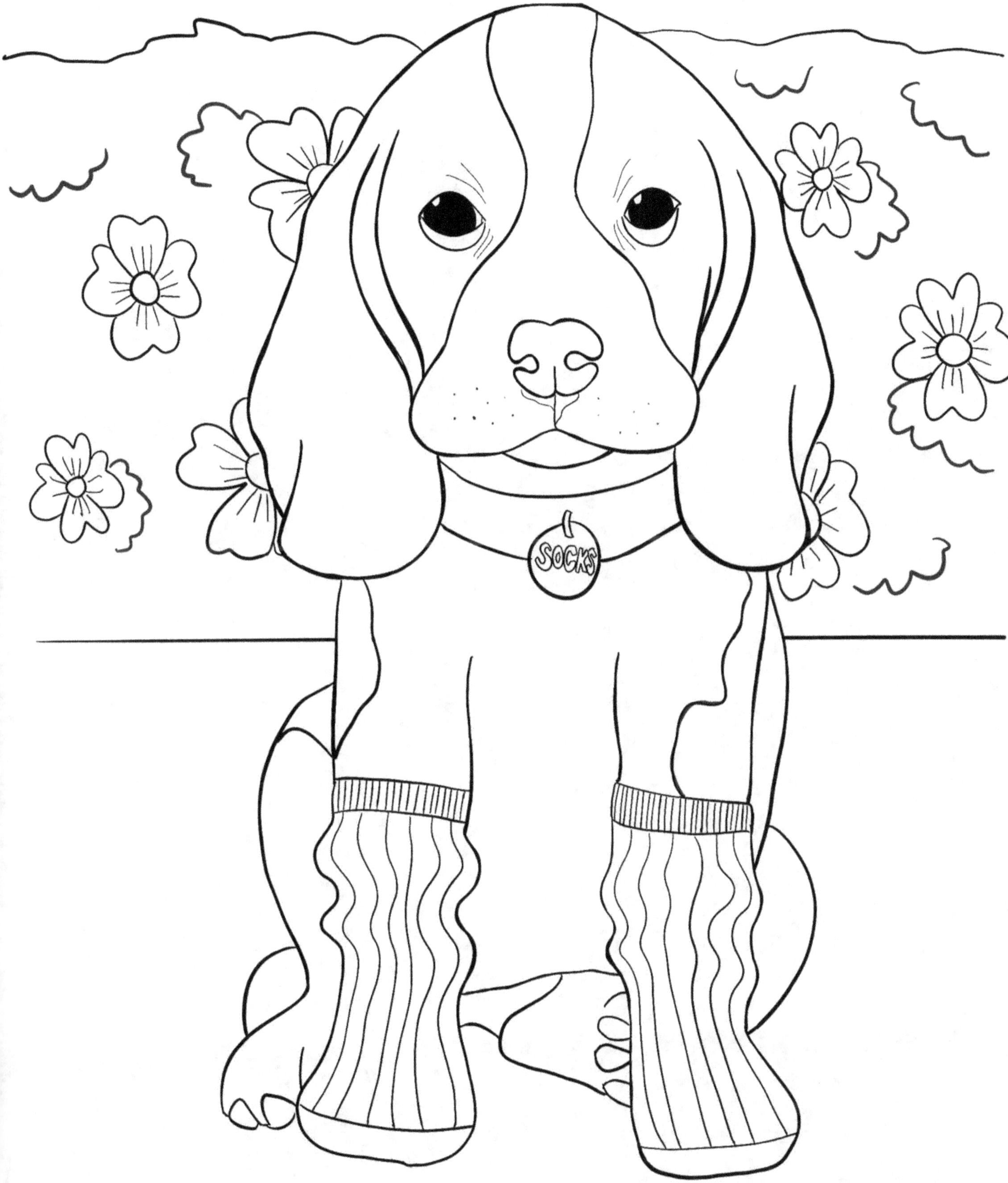
SOCKS

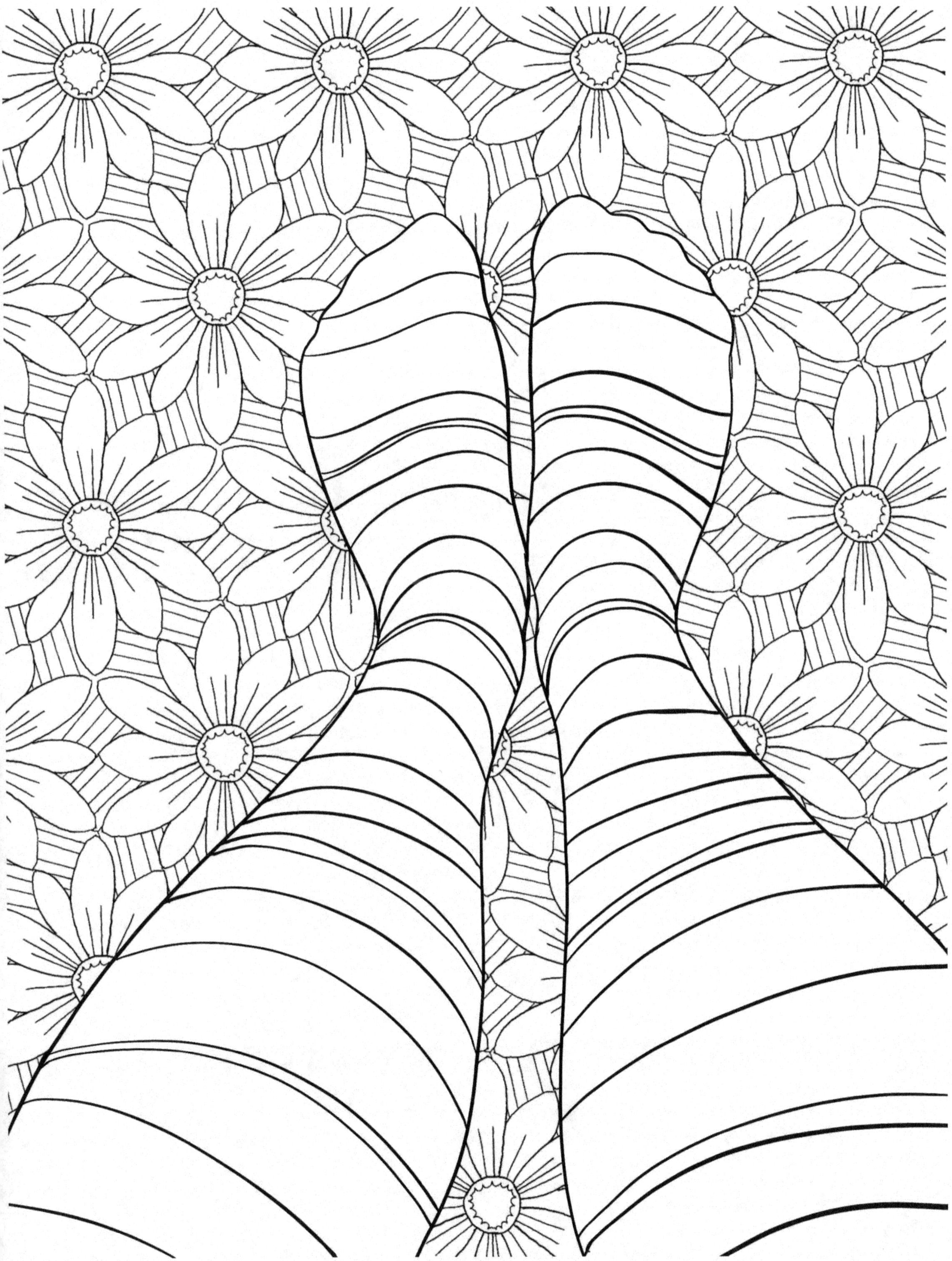

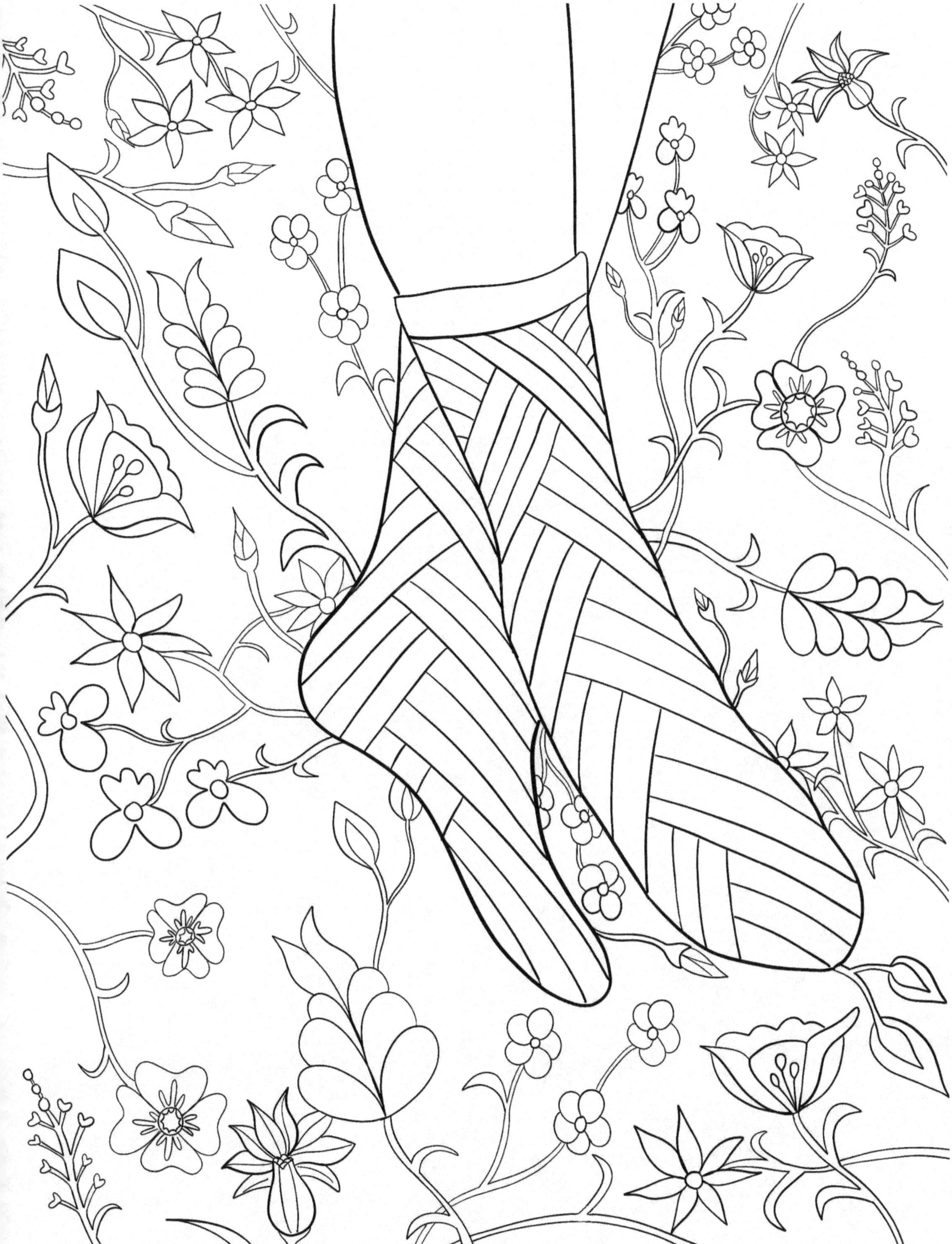

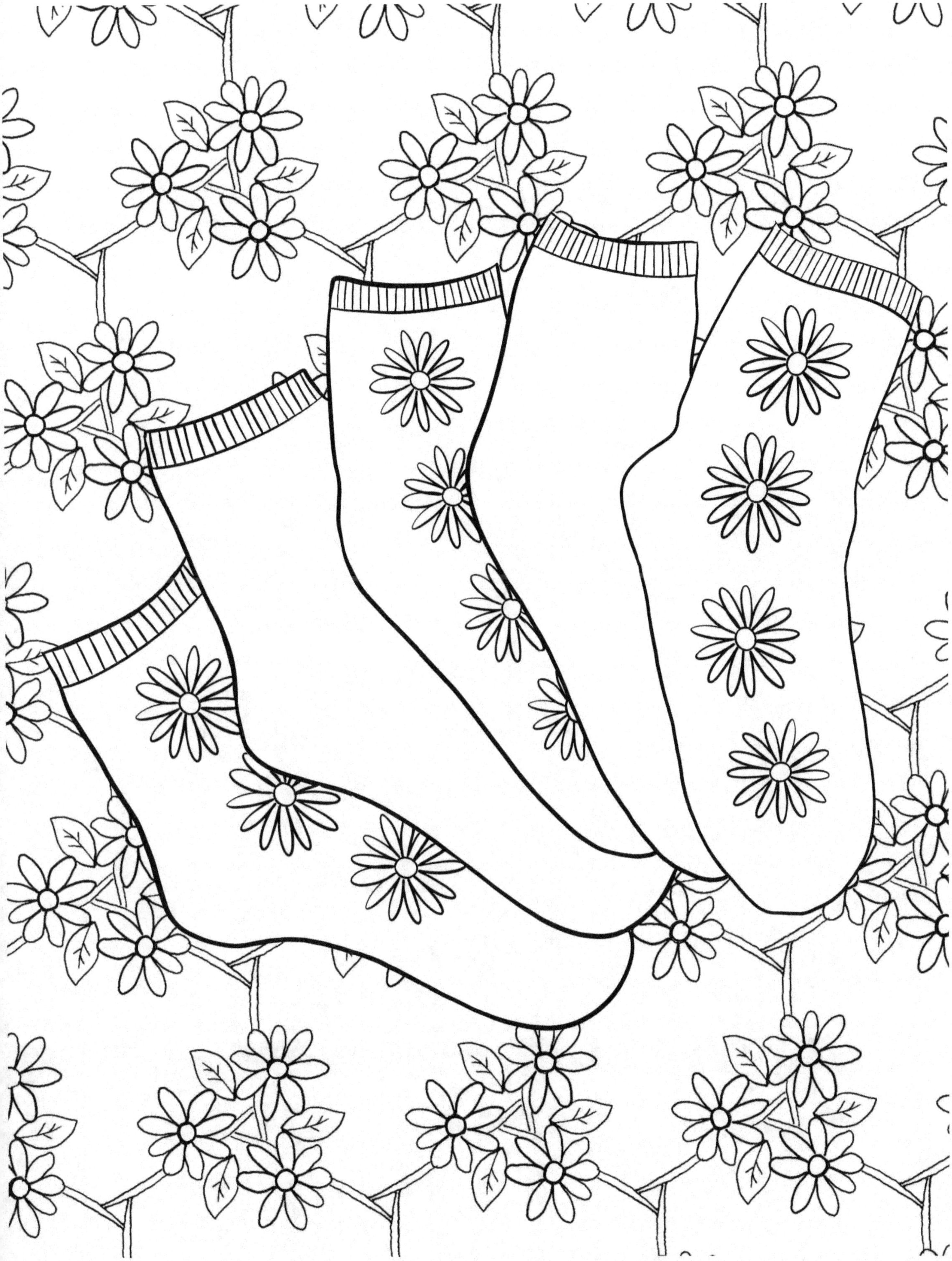

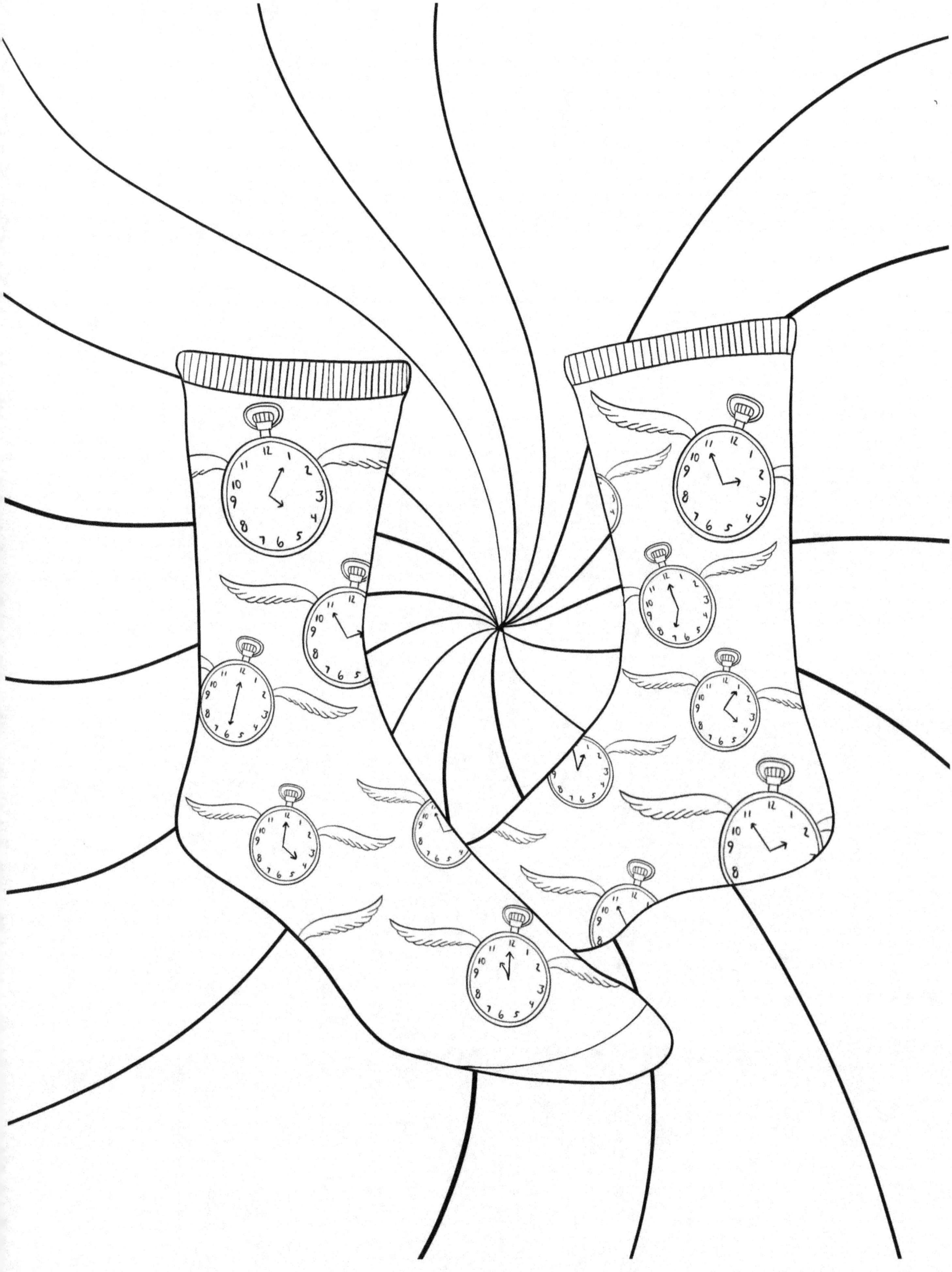

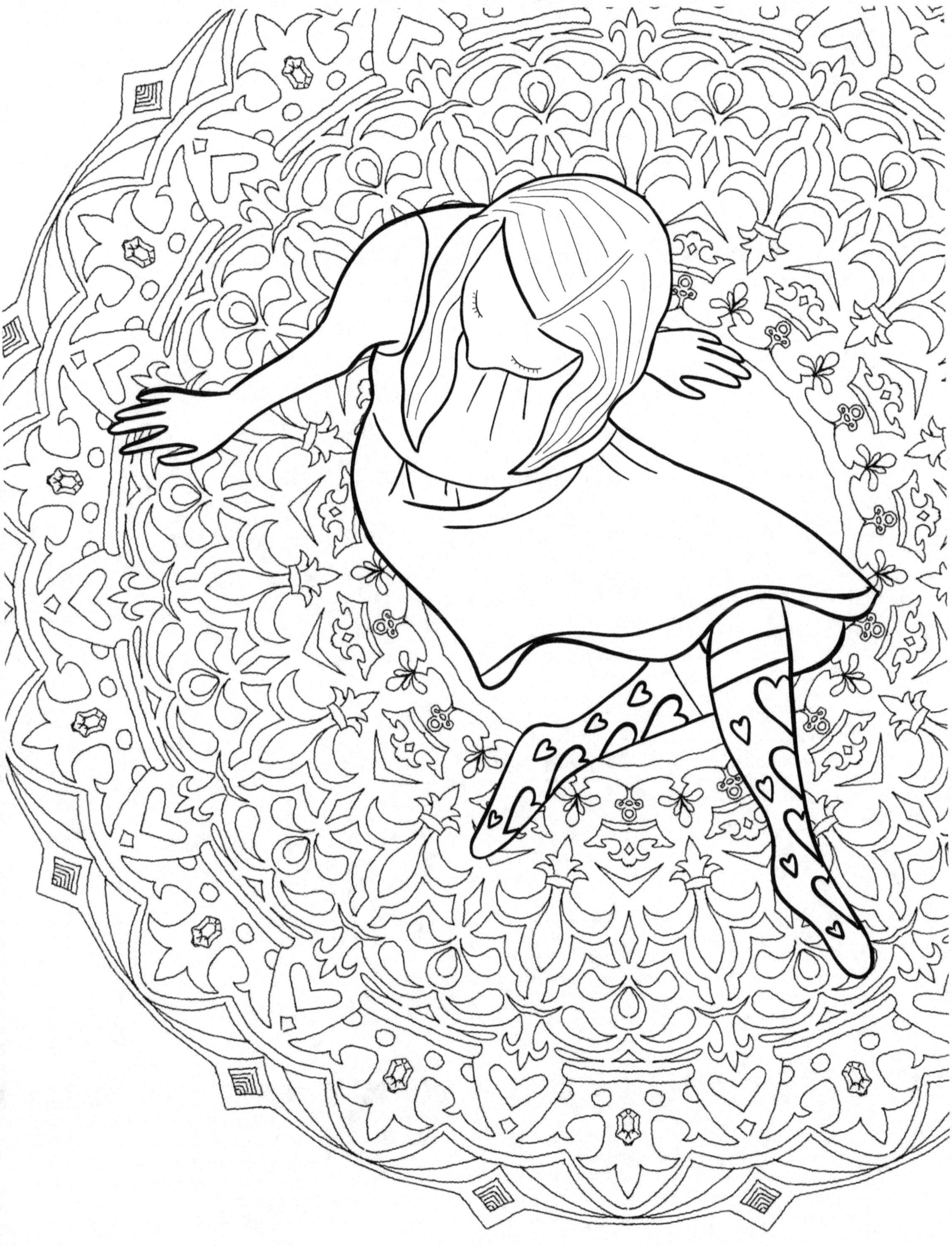

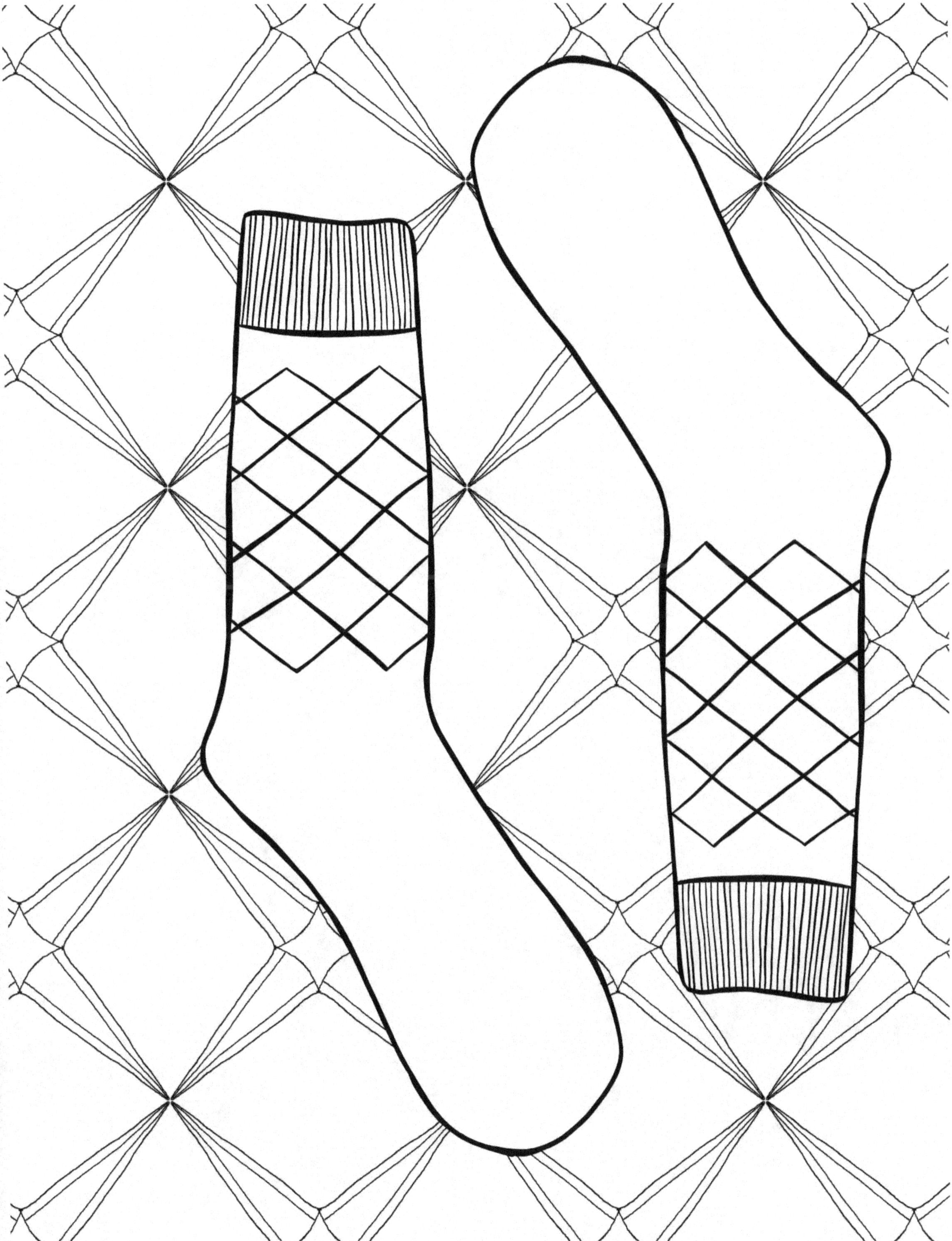

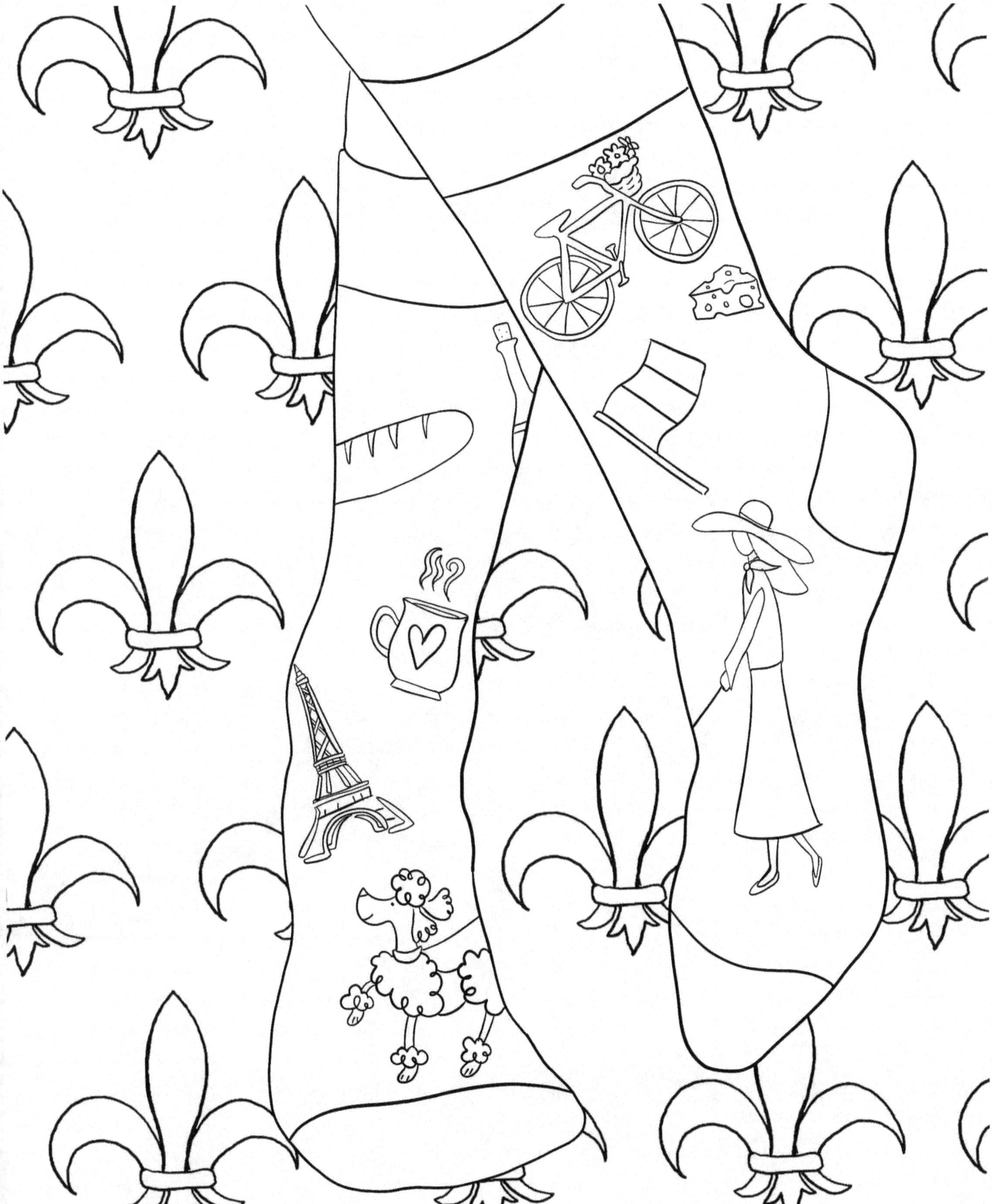

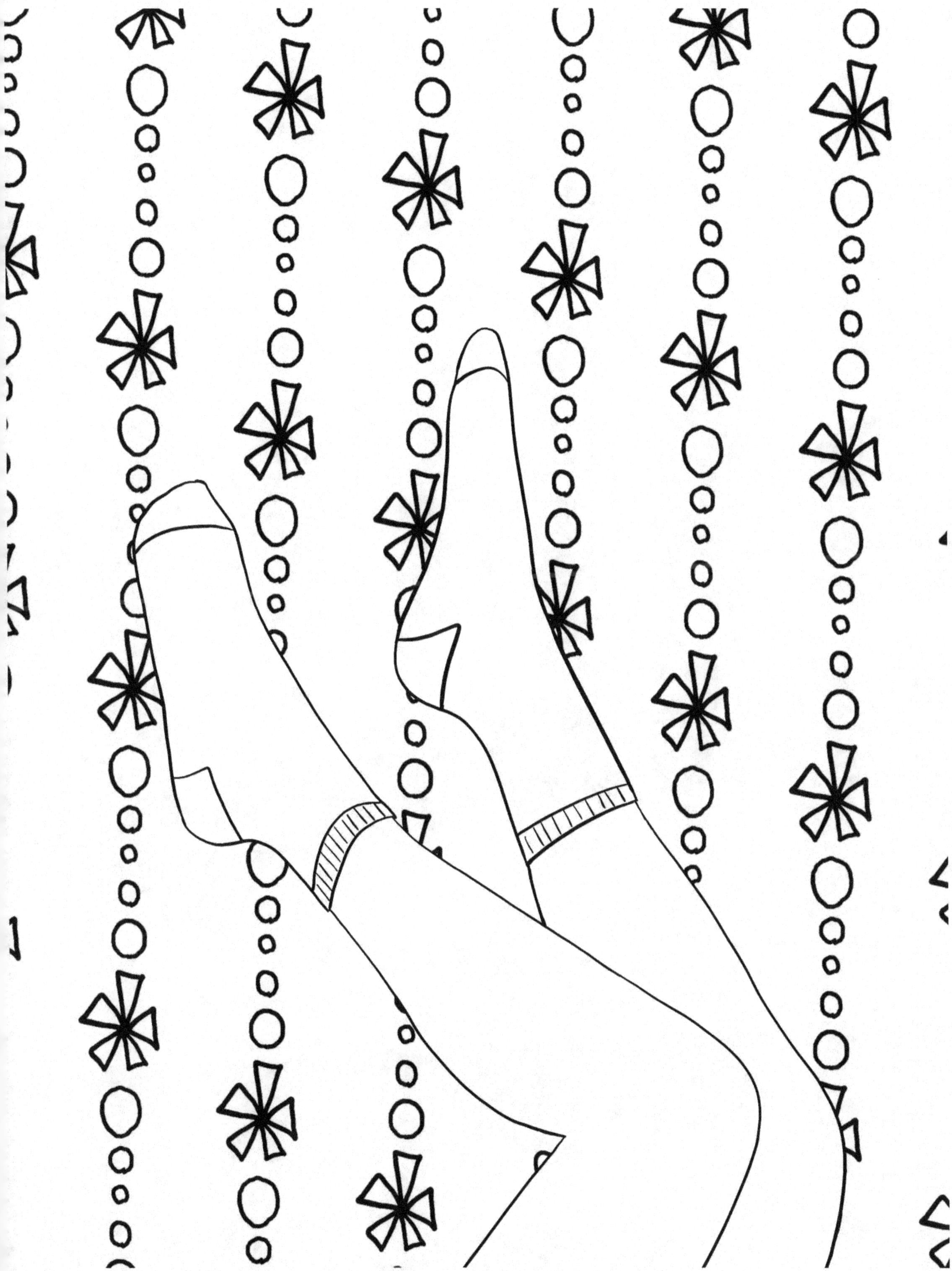

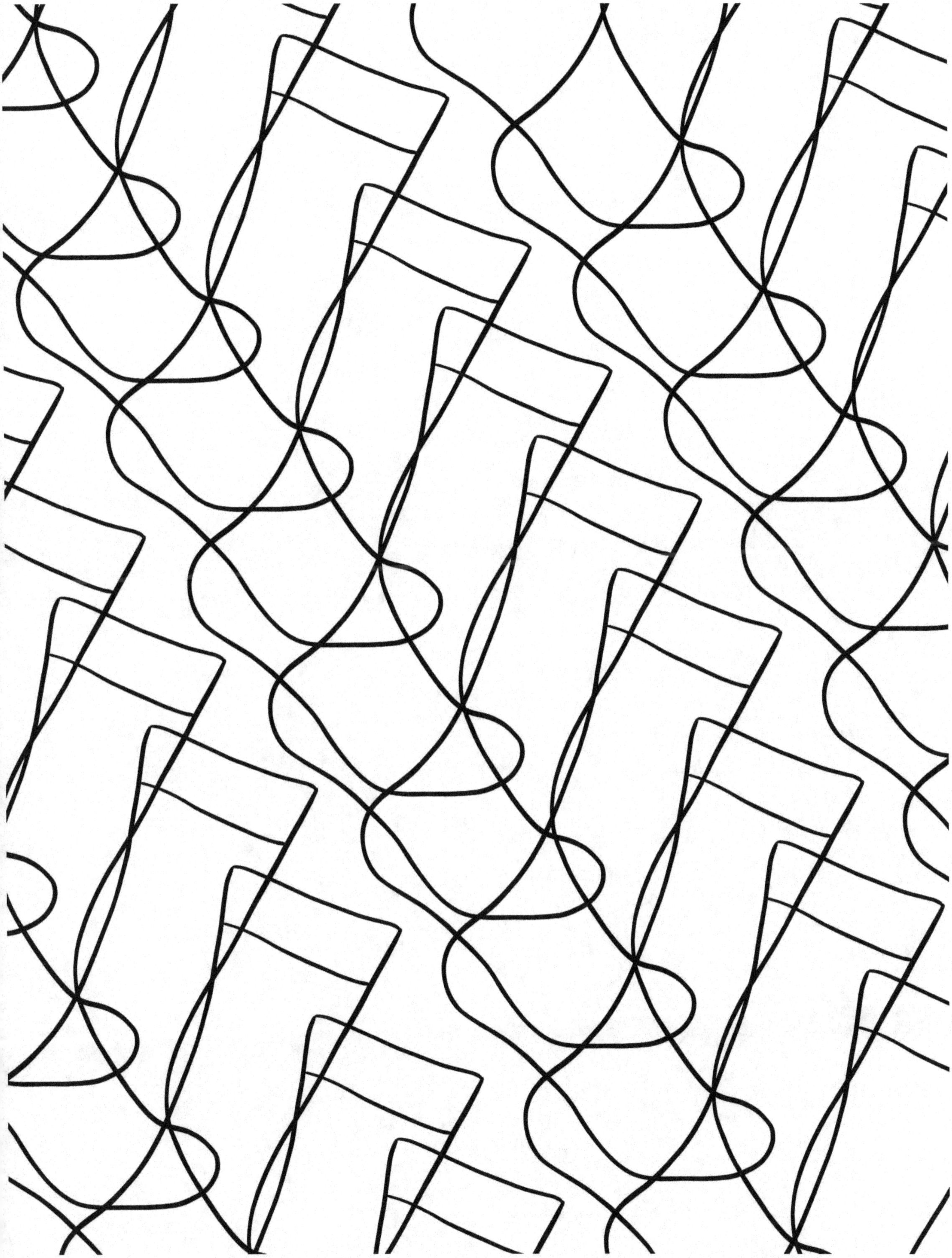

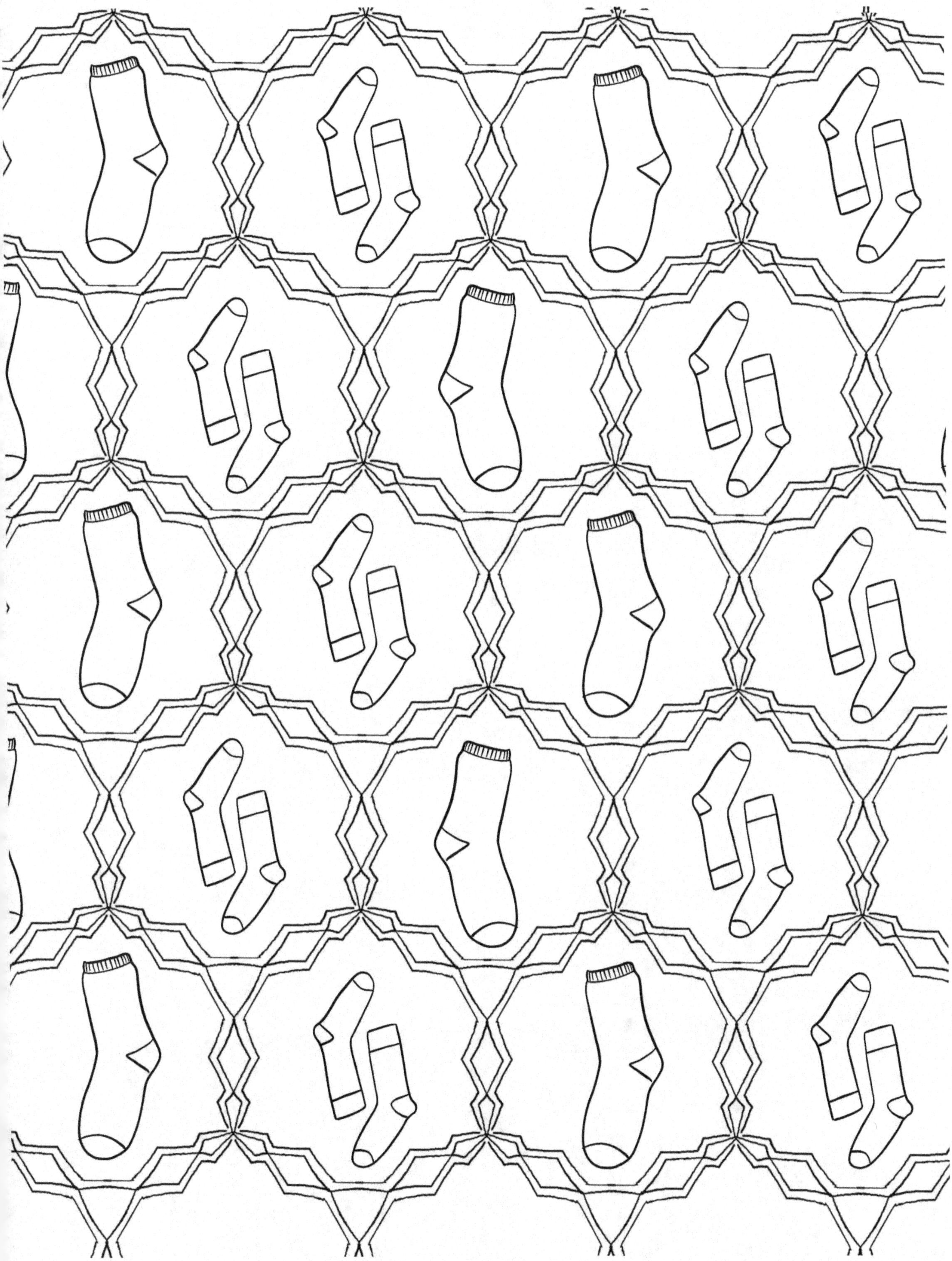

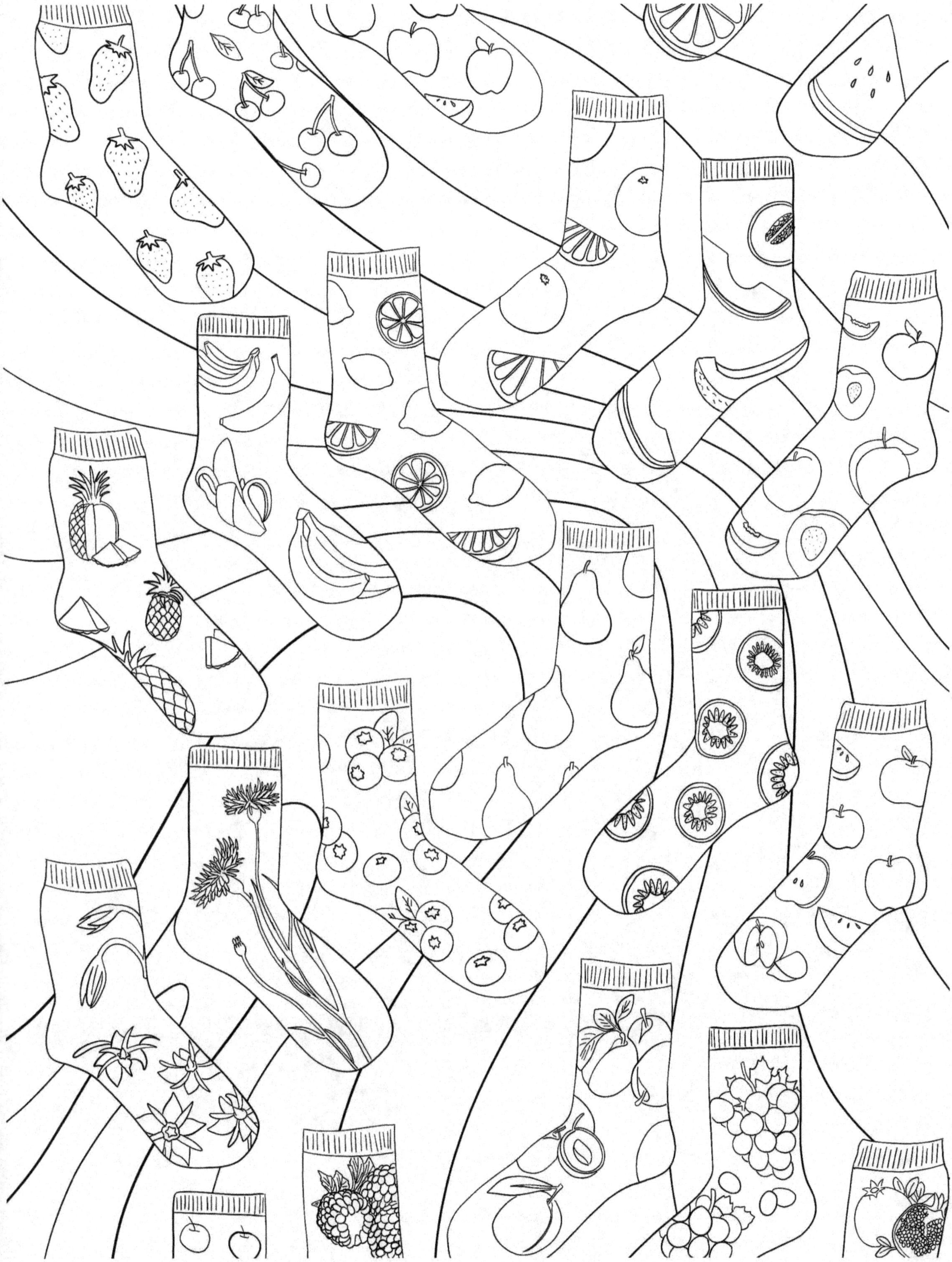

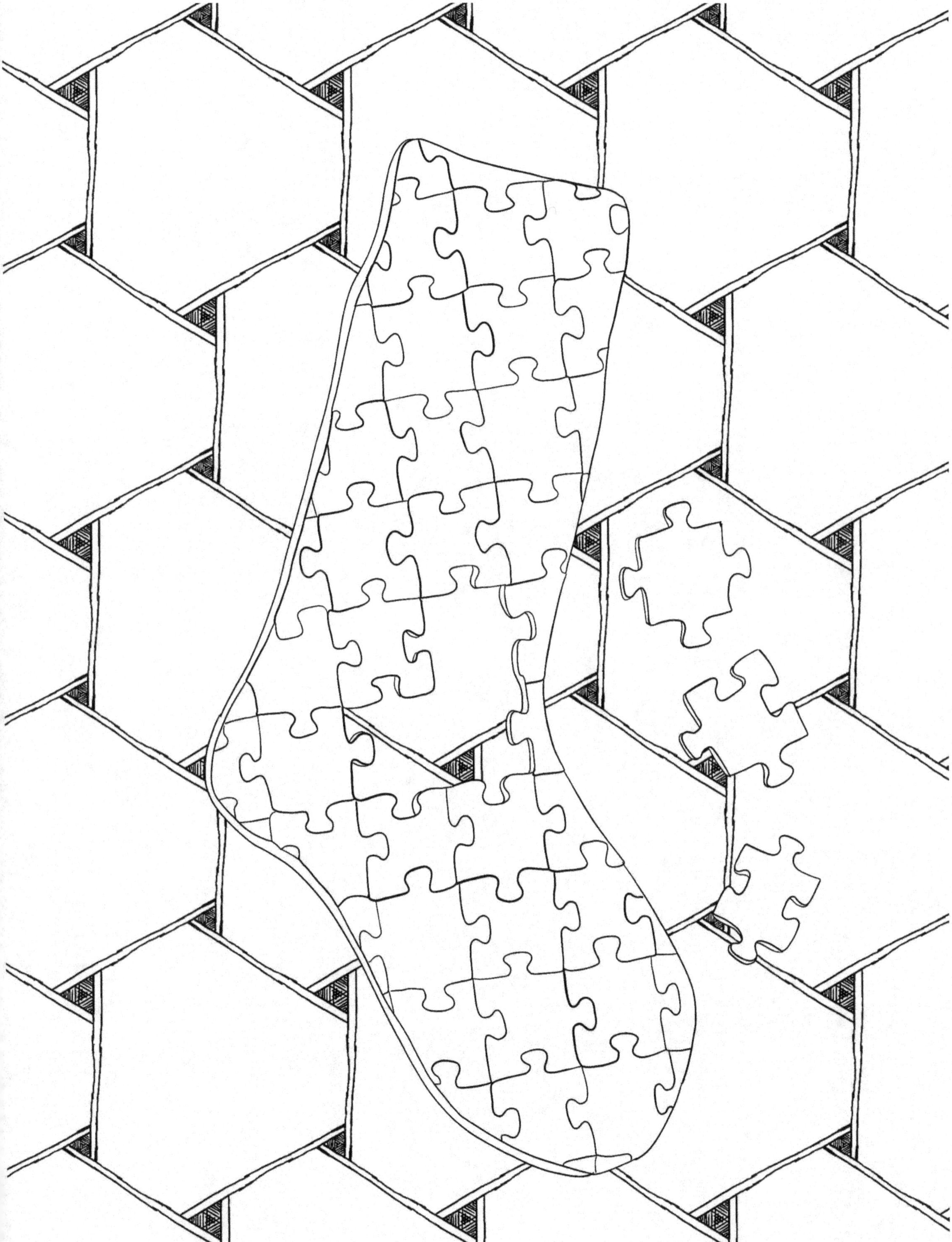

www.ingramcontent.com/pod-product-compliance
Lightning Source LLC
Chambersburg PA
CBHW081211170526
45165CB00009B/2787